THE
SUNDERLA
AFC
MISCELLANY

THE
SUNDERLAND
AFC
MISCELLANY

PAUL DAYS

To my wife Beverley and my children Harry and Millie.
'Get off the computer Daddy!'

First published 2009

The History Press
The Mill, Brimscombe Port
Stroud, Gloucestershire, GL5 2QG
www.thehistorypress.co.uk

© Paul Days, 2009

The right of Paul Days to be identified as the Author
of this work has been asserted in accordance with the
Copyrights, Designs and Patents Act 1988.

British Library Cataloguing in Publication Data.
A catalogue record for this book is available from the British Library.

ISBN 978 0 7524 5336 1

Typesetting and origination by The History Press
Printed in Malta

CONTENTS

ACKNOWLEDGEMENTS

Thanks to anyone who ever wrote or uttered a single word on Sunderland Football Club. Without the conversations, newspapers, books, annuals and anecdotes, this publication wouldn't be possible.

Thanks to Sunderland AFC who afforded me a glimpse behind the scenes from 1995 to 2002. Thanks also to the supporters of Sunderland AFC whose humour, in the face of footballing adversity, has made the long journey worthwhile. In particular Graeme, Twinny, Cosher, Alan, Brian (RIP), Woody (RIP), Emby, Martyn and A Love Supreme, The Ready To Go Message Board, Dave Harrison, Rob Mason, Tommy Lynn, the Chester-le-Street Supporters Branch, and George Hoare; in fact too many to name. You know who you are. I always appreciate the support and backing I have received in my football writing from friends, family and of course the Sunderland fans themselves.

Finally, thanks to Sunderland historian Dave Hillam who is no longer with us. RIP.

Paul Days

FOREWORD

by Gary Bennett

It is with great pleasure that I write the foreword to *The Sunderland AFC Miscellany* – a club that I have been associated with for 25 years.

I joined Sunderland AFC from Cardiff City for £65,000 in the summer of 1984 and I could never have dreamed that I would enjoy such a close and long association with a football club that, as Niall Quinn has stated, quickly gets under your skin.

To become, eventually, fifth-highest in the list of appearances for Sunderland AFC, one of the oldest, most famous, traditional and historic football clubs in the United Kingdom is indeed an honour and one that I am very proud of. To be captain was a very special feeling.

Who would have thought that a young lad from Manchester would become an adopted Mackem, making my home in the north-east where I now enjoy a close rapport with individuals within the region, my fellow professionals who have worn the famous red and white striped shirt and, of course, the mass of people who support Sunderland AFC.

Having read the book, it strikes me that although a football club is of course about what happens on the field of play, what happens off it also defines their character and it is humbling to be part of an institution that had such beginnings in Hendon, a very close-knit part of the city, where of course Raich Carter was born.

The stories are fascinating, many light-hearted and some of the statistical information is illuminating. My own miscellaneous fact is that I scored on my Sunderland first team debut against Southampton at Roker Park, a game that we won 3–1. The goalkeeper incidentally was Peter Shilton, widely regarded as the best goalkeeper in the world at the time. However, he was unable to stop my powerful 2-yard tap in!

Finally, my only disappointment with the Sunderland fans, with whom I have enjoyed such a rapport, was that when David Speedie landed in the Clock Stand Paddock I was hoping he would stay there. Why did you throw him back out?

Enjoy the book.

Gary Bennett, August 2009

THEY SAID IT...

'Soccer is the biggest thing that's happened in creation, bigger than any "ism" you can name'

Alan Brown, Sunderland manager, 1968

'I wouldn't trust some of these people to walk my dog.'

Roy Keane, former Sunderland manager, on the TV pundits

'We don't just need points now, we need snookers!'

Bob Murray, Sunderland AFC chairman on Sunderland's chances of avoiding the drop

'We have got to get away from that relegation area as quickly as possible as it's not good for anybody's health.'

Howard Wilkinson before going on an unhealthy run of two wins in twenty-two games

'There was the drama of strong men weeping.'

Albert McInroy on Billy Williams' last game as Sunderland trainer in 1928. Williams had been at the club since 1897

'I can't wait to meet Roy Keane; I've got a few of his qualities but I would never claim to be half as hard as he is!'

England cricketer and Sunderland fan Paul Collingwood looks forward to meeting 'Keano'

THE JOKE'S ON US

Supporting Sunderland doesn't come with a 'Glory Boy' tag. Throughout our ups and downs we can at least laugh at ourselves. It's best not to take it all too seriously.

A couple in the middle of a messy divorce case find themselves in court battling over custody of little Johnny, their only child. In order to make a fair decision over the boy's future, the Judge takes Johnny into his private chambers so that he can find out which of the parents the boy would prefer to live with.

'Well, Johnny' said the Judge, 'Would you like to live with your Mother?'

'No,' replied Johnny, 'she hits me all the time.'

'Well then,' the Judge continues, 'Would you like to live with your Father?'

'No,' replied Johnny again, 'He hits me all the time too!'

The Judge looks exasperated and says to the boy, 'Well Johnny, who would you like to live with?'

'I'd like to live with Sunderland Football Club,' the boy replied quickly.

'Why on earth would you want to live with Sunderland Football Club?' asked the now extremely puzzled Judge.

'Well' replied Johnny, 'They never beat anyone!'

British Rail has decided to start sponsoring Sunderland. BR thinks they are a suitable team because of their regular points failures.

NON LEAGUE SUCCESS

Since entering the Football League in 1890 Sunderland have been knocked out of the FA Cup by non league opposition four times:

Tottenham Hotspur	1–2	1898/99
New Brompton	1–3	1907/08
Norwich City	1–3	1910/11
Yeovil Town	1–2	1949/50

In total Sunderland have played 22 matches against non league opposition in the FA Cup, including replays, winning 15.

ANIMAL CRACKERS

On 20 December 1884 Sunderland recorded their biggest ever victory when they defeated Castletown 23–0. Commenting on the game in 1931, Sunderland founder John Grayston indicated that Hylton's Colonel Briggs, who had proposed the challenge match, watched as 'his Sister rode round the field on horseback to cheer her Brother on.' The reaction of the Sunderland players isn't recorded!

In January 1909, Sunderland were going through what was for them a relatively lean spell. It had been seven years since they had won the League, and the team which was to win the Championship with a record number of points and get to the Cup Final in 1913 was only just starting to come together. A 4–1 home defeat to Liverpool on New Year's Day 1909 left the club in the bottom half of the First Division. When the players came into the dressing room the following day, before the game against Bury, they found a stray black cat in residence.

On 18 September 1909, the league encounter with Newcastle United on Wearside was remembered for all the wrong reasons. At the Fulwell End the crowd spilled onto the pitch, there were some 40,000 present, a Roker Park record at that time. As the playing area was being cleared, which took 15 minutes to do so, a police horse was stabbed. The match was repeatedly delayed and at one point abandonment was definitely on the cards.

In March 1958 Sunderland signed Don Kitchenbrand from Glasgow Rangers. The Ibrox faithful had nicknamed the South African 'Rhino' because of his physique and no-nonsense style of play. The name stayed with him for his time on Wearside.

On 10 December 1977, Tottenham Hotspur travelled north to play Sunderland at Roker Park. Bad feeling brewed between the fans and in the second half the Spurs fans ran onto the pitch to escape their marauding hosts. It took the intervention of a police horse at the Roker End of the pitch to restore order. The match was televised on *Match of the Day*.

On 14 January 1978, Sunderland travelled to London to play Leyton Orient. The game was eventful for three things: Sunderland's goalkeeper Barry Siddall was ordered from the field to change his red goalkeeper's shirt that clashed with the home side, Gary Rowell missed his only competitive penalty kick for the Black Cats and a dog ran on the pitch holding up the play.

THERE IS NO SUBSTITUTE FOR ...

Daniele Dichio, the Sunderland forward, signed from the Genoa-based Italian side Sampdoria. He was a named substitute no fewer than ninety-two times during his Wearside career, a club record.

SCORING SENSATION

Arthur Bridgett signed for Sunderland from Stoke City in January 1903. From the 30 March 1907 away game at Everton until the 7 September 1907 home game with Notts County, Bridgett scored in all 9 consecutive games; a club record, notching a total of ten goals.

Coming a close second was goalscorer par excellence Johnny Campbell who notched in 8 successive games during the early 1890s, scoring a total of 17 goals in the process.

GROUNDS FOR OPTIMISM

The Stadium of Light, Sunderland's present ground, is their seventh home. The others in chronological order are:

Blue House Field, Hendon	1879 to 1881
Groves Field, Ashbrooke	1882 to 1883
Horatio Street, Roker	1883 to 1884
Abbs Field, Fulwell	1884 to 1886
Newcastle Road	1886 to 1898
Roker Park	1898 to 1997

FOUNDING FATHER

Sunderland AFC were formed by a Scotsman, James Allan. Allan was born in Ayrshire sometime in 1858 and had attended Glasgow University where he studied, prior to coming down to Sunderland to take up a teaching position at Hendon Board

School. At the school he was the Second Assistant Master, appointed in April 1879 at a salary of £60, rising to £90.

James Allan was a complex and often unpopular character but successful in his teaching career; so much so that on leaving Hendon Board School he moved on to teaching at Thomas Street School, finally becoming the Headmaster of Hylton Road School until his death in 1911.

He took an active part in football all of his life, holding the position of Treasurer at the time he left Sunderland AFC, and then of course leading the breakaway that formed Sunderland Albion in 1888, a move that almost saw the death of Sunderland AFC. He was also at one point the chairman of the Wearside League.

He was always a very fit man and attempted to cycle from Sunderland to Glasgow to witness the 5 April 1890 Scotland v. England encounter at Hampden Park. He was thwarted when his bike gave up on him at Edinburgh!

As a player he was notionally an outside left and was a prolific goalscorer. To prove this he holds the clubs individual goalscoring record of 12 in one match, against Castletown in 1884. However, to counter this he was very often accused of dishing out 'rough play' on the opposition in a needless, underhand way. He could be a selfish ball player which often left his team mates exasperated. Due to his slight physique he was often referred to as 'The Boneless Wonder'.

However, his footballing exploits were enough for him to be recognised by The Rangers club from Newcastle, for example, who recruited Allan to play for them against the then mighty Queens Park from Glasgow in the 1882/83 season. Although The Rangers team lost, James Allan 'raised cheer after cheer by his determined play, dribbling nearly the whole length of the field time after time.'

In the 1884/85 seasons Allan was accused of bribing one of the Birtley backs, Watson, to the tune of £2 to 'play a dummy game.' Incensed, Allan threatened legal action, in his usual straight to the point, go for the jugular manner. No further action was pursued by Birtley.

Although Allan played in many friendly and Durham Challenge Cup games for Sunderland, his record shows that he featured in just 3 competitive fixtures for the club, all FA

Cup ties, including the club's very first professional match which was the Redcar cup tie in November 1884. He also gained representative honours with both County Durham and Northumberland.

James Allan died on 18 October 1911 at his home, 37 Elmwood Street, Sunderland. The death certificate gives his occupation on the date of death as a School Master. His passing was registered in the Sunderland West Sub-District by his son W. Allan on the day he died, with the cause of death given by James Chalmers MD as Apoplexy. This is a general medical term given to someone who passes away very quickly from, for example, a sudden heart attack. Therefore we know that the club's founder did not suffer in his passing. Allan was just fifty-three years old.

To form one prominent team wasn't enough for Allan; he formed two and in doing so left himself as an integral part of the sporting history of the City of Sunderland. Football-wise he sits alongside Charles Alcock as one of the finest and most influential sports administrators the city has ever produced. Considering Alcock is widely regarded as The Father of Modern Sport, this is some feat by Allan.

ROLE REVERSAL

Southampton were the last team to defeat Sunderland at Roker Park and Sunderland were the last team to defeat Southampton at The Dell.

IN A HURRY

The highest ever away win in the history of top flight English league football occurred when Sunderland travelled to St James' Park in December 1908 and inflicted a 9–1 defeat on arch-rivals Newcastle United. Six of the Sunderland goals were scored in a blistering 15-minute second-half spell. The half-time score had been 1–1. Two Sunderland players scored hat-tricks that day: Billy Hogg and George Holley.

FOR THE BENEFIT OF?

In the days before the modern term 'testimonial' was used to refer to awarding games to players who had been with a club for ten years, they were termed 'benefit' matches (and you didn't necessarily have to be with the same club for ten years). The first of such benefit matches to be awarded to a Sunderland player was on 27 November 1886 when Sunderland entertained Newcastle West End. Dowk Oliver was the recipient having broken his collar bone in a previous English cup tie between the two teams.

The only players to have been awarded two benefit matches by Sunderland are Harry Low and Charlie Buchan. The second of Low's benefit games was posthumous as he died aged just thirty-eight. The match was for the benefit of his widow and children.

CHAMPIONS!

Sunderland AFC have been English League Champions on six occasions – 1891/92, 1892/93, 1894/95, 1901/02, 1912/13 and 1935/36. Despite not having won the title in over seventy years there are still only five clubs who can beat Sunderland's record of six. Below is the list of those five clubs together with the number of titles they have won and the year they obtained their seventh English Championship – i.e. to beat Sunderland's record:

Liverpool	18	1965/66
Manchester United	18	1966/67
Arsenal	13	1952/53
Everton	9	1969/70
Aston Villa	7	1980/81

COULDN'T SCORE

Ernie England played 351 games for Sunderland AFC between 1919 and 1930. He never scored a solitary goal. This is a club record for an outfield player.

HOME SWEET HOME

Arsenal didn't defeat Sunderland on Wearside in 14 league visits from 1968 to 2001.

Aston Villa won only twice in 26 league visits to Sunderland from 1891 to 1919.

From 1913 to 1948 Bolton Wanderers were without a league win on Wearside from their 22 visits, conceding 73 goals.

Derby County have won only 3 games on Wearside in their last 33 attempts, dating back to 1935.

Since 1958 Sunderland have defeated Liverpool once in their last 24 league visits to Wearside.

From 1965 to 2000 Manchester United won only 2 of 15 league games they played on Wearside.

Middlesbrough defeated Sunderland in only 3 of their first 46 league visits to Wearside.

From 1908 to 1980 Nottingham Forest went 19 league games without winning on Wearside.

Portsmouth won 4–1 at Roker Park in 1949. Their next league win on Wearside would come in 1985, 20 visits later.

From 1891 to 1936 Preston North End played Sunderland on Wearside for league points 29 times. They never won a single game.

Since 1924 Sheffield United has visited Sunderland 36 times playing for league points. They have won only 3 times, conceding 89 goals.

Stoke City lost 21 of their first 22 league visits to Sunderland.

FOUR IN A ROW

There are only five clubs who have won on four consecutive league visits to Wearside:

Everton	1915 to 1921
Leeds United	1990 to 2000
Liverpool	1985 to 1999
Liverpool	2002 to 2008
Norwich City	1985 to 1997
Southend United	1991 to 1994

Only Liverpool have won five consecutive league games on Wearside – 1969 to 1981.

WELL TRAVELLED

Sunderland have won on five successive league visits to the following clubs:

Bradford City	1990 to 2003
Manchester United	1949 to 1952
Newcastle United	1899 to 1903
West Bromwich Albion	1890 to 1894

SUNDERLAND ARE WORLD CHAMPIONS!

On 27 April 1895, Sunderland became 'World Champions'. It was customary at the time for the Scottish League champions to take on the English league champions and as both countries were pre-eminent in football at the time, the fixtures were billed as a World Championship.

The Sunderland team left the North-East shortly after 8 a.m. and arrived in Edinburgh at 12.45 p.m. to take on Heart of Midlothian. Sunderland lunched at the Douglas Hotel and prior to the 4 o'clock kick off took a stroll. The weather was poor, but that didn't dampen the enthusiasm of the 10,000 spectators who were treated to an excellent game of football with the match ending 5–3 in Sunderland's favour.

DERAILED

Sunderland's top 20 worst away defeats in league competition are as follows:

26/12/1911	FL1	A	The Wednesday	L	0–8
19/10/1968	FL1	A	West Ham	L	0–8
25/9/1982	FL1	A	Watford	L	0–8
22/3/1909	FL1	A	Blackburn Rovers	L	1–8
19/11/1955	FL1	A	Luton Town	L	2–8
5/10/1957	FL1	A	Blackpool	L	0–7
30/9/1893	FL1	A	Everton	L	1–7
21/11/1914	FL1	A	Everton	L	1–7
8/2/1958	FL1	A	Luton Town	L	1–7
24/11/2007	PL	A	Everton	L	1–7
28/11/1903	FL1	A	Derby County	L	2–7
1/11/1930	FL1	A	Sheffield Wed	L	2–7
3/9/1955	FL1	A	Blackpool	L	3–7
28/3/1936	FL1	A	Middlesbrough	L	0–6
12/4/1937	FL1	A	Grimsby Town	L	0–6
3/11/1956	FL1	A	Preston NE	L	0–6
12/10/1957	FL1	A	Burnley	L	0–6
17/9/1958	FL2	A	Sheffield Wed	L	0–6
30/3/1959	FL2	A	Leyton Orient	L	0–6
11/10/1992	FL1	A	West Ham	L	0–6

PUT TO THE SWORD

Sunderland AFC's top 20 league home victories are as follows:

1/9/1894	FL1	H	Derby County	W	8–0
22/10/1892	FL1	H	WBA	W	8–1
1/9/1956	FL1	H	Charlton Athletic	W	8–1
4/2/1931	FL1	H	Blackburn Rovers	W	8–2
12/12/1891	FL1	H	Darwen	W	7–0
7/12/1912	FL1	H	Liverpool	W	7–0
26/12/1934	FL1	H	Everton	W	7–0
3/11/1987	FL3	H	Southend United	W	7–0

19/9/1998	FL1	H	Oxford United	W	7–0
14/11/1891	FL1	H	Derby County	W	7–1
8/12/1894	FL1	H	Small Heath	W	7–1
25/1/1896	FL1	H	WBA	W	7–1
6/10/1926	FL1	H	Burnley	W	7–1
11/4/1952	FL1	H	Huddersfield Town	W	7–1
12/9/1953	FL1	H	Arsenal	W	7–1
31/12/1960	FL2	H	Luton Town	W	7–1
20/3/1963	FL2	H	Norwich City	W	7–1
12/1/1901	FL1	H	Wolverhampton W	W	7–2
10/3/1906	FL1	H	Wolverhampton W	W	7–2
7/3/1908	FL1	H	Nottingham Forest	W	7–2

TOP TRAVELLERS

Sunderland's top 20 away victories in league competition are as follows:

5/12/1908	FL1	A	Newcastle United	W	9–1
23/4/1892	FL1	A	Darwen	W	7–1
13/4/1936	FL1	A	Birmingham	W	7–2
3/9/1892	FL1	A	Accrington	W	6–0
19/12/1914	FL1	A	Tottenham H	W	6–0
19/4/1930	FL1	A	Liverpool	W	6–0
17/9/1892	FL1	A	Aston Villa	W	6–1
9/9/1933	FL1	A	Wolverhampton W	W	6–1
23/10/1937	FL1	A	WBA	W	6–1
3/12/1892	FL1	A	Nottingham Forest	W	5–0
4/3/1893	FL1	A	Newton Heath	W	5–0
18/1/1947	FL1	A	Blackpool	W	5–0
18/9/1999	PL	A	Derby County	W	5–0
6/5/2007	FL1	A	Luton Town	W	5–0
2/11/1912	FL1	A	Bradford City	W	5–1
15/11/1913	FL1	A	Everton	W	5–1
12/2/1921	FL1	A	Aston Villa	W	5–1
16/11/1935	FL1	A	Brentford	W	5–1
25/10/1890	FL1	A	Bolton Wanderers	W	5–2
17/10/1891	FL1	A	WBA	W	5–2

HOME DEFEATS

Sunderland's top 20 worst home defeats in league competition are as follows:

26/12/1955	FL1	H	Newcastle United	L	1–6
5/4/1958	FL1	H	Birmingham City	L	1–6
26/12/1938	FL1	H	Aston Villa	L	1–5
1/1/1966	FL1	H	WBA	L	1–5
9/9/1967	FL1	H	West Ham	L	1–5
7/11/1981	FL1	H	Manchester United	L	1–5
2/9/1907	FL1	H	Manchester City	L	2–5
1/1/1927	FL1	H	Blackburn Rovers	L	2–5
25/12/1930	FL1	H	Leicester City	L	2–5
2/1/1932	FL1	H	Manchester City	L	2–5
20/4/1907	FL1	H	Bury	L	3–5
11/4/1923	FL1	H	Sheffield United	L	3–5
29/8/1953	FL1	H	Manchester City	L	4–5
13/11/1965	FL1	H	Burnley	L	0–4
21/9/1968	FL1	H	Manchester City	L	0–4
27/8/1969	FL1	H	Manchester City	L	0–4
13/2/1971	FL2	H	Cardiff City	L	0–4
8/12/1984	FL1	H	Leicester City	L	0–4
4/5/1985	FL1	H	Aston Villa	L	0–4
4/3/1997	PL	H	Tottenham Hotspur	L	0–4

THEY SAID IT ...

'I can remember it like it was yesterday. It was May 1973. QPR's game at Sunderland had been delayed, because of the cup final, which Sunderland had won that year with a flukey win against Leeds, the best team in the country. We had to play them the Monday afterwards. They paraded the Cup around their ground and then they left it on a table on the halfway line. A guy called Tony Hazel and I had a little bet who could hit it with the ball. It was just a spontaneous thing. I did it during the warm-up and it didn't go down very well. I ran straight across the park and then, bang! the FA Cup goes shooting up in the air. I believe it got dented, but I don't know whether Hazel done it or I did; it doesn't really matter though. Once it was done it was done.

During the match I was winding up all their players, who had probably had a few drinks over the weekend. We beat them 3–0. I scored two goals and almost caused a riot by taking the piss. I was going up to their players and asking them, 'How the f**k did you ever beat f***ing Leeds?' It was the headlines on the *News at 10* – we had to be taken off the pitch for about half an hour. All their fans ran on the pitch and delayed the end of the game.

I was playing really well at the time and it was a nuisance having to go up to Sunderland on a Monday night for the last game of the season. It was an easy win and when on form I could be a bit arrogant. As far as I can recall, it was just after half time when all the Sunderland people jumped over the fence and ran on to the pitch and we had to be taken off. They just came from behind the goal like a swarm. Some of them were coming at me but luckily enough I was right near the touchline and I managed to get off quick and into the dressing room. It was like a load of wildebeest coming at you.

Our chairman, Jim Gregory, wanted to call the game off but we had to go back out after 40 minutes. We didn't go out on the town after the game, that's for sure. Not that I had any interest in going out in Sunderland anyway. We stayed in the hotel and just drank, but the next day we had to get a police escort up to the station. It got out of hand – I didn't know they were all mad up there. I've never spoken to any of the Sunderland players – put it this way, I won't be doing any work in Sunderland. I know a lot of people in Newcastle and they tell me, 'Don't go to Sunderland Stan, they've got long memories and they don't like you.'

Queens Park Rangers' attacking maestro Stan Bowles on the mutual bad feeling after he knocked the FA Cup off its stand at Roker Park in 1973 following the FA Cup Final, and ran the show as the visitors won 3–0, prompting a pitch invasion by the Sunderland fans

GOALS, GOALS, GOALS!

Here are the league games featuring the most goals:

6/12/1930	FL1	H	Liverpool	W	6–5
29/10/1932	FL1	H	Bolton Wanderers	W	7–4
24/3/1934	FL1	A	WBA	L	5–6
16/12/1950	FL1	A	Derby County	L	5–6
19/1/1907	FL1	H	Liverpool	D	5–5
10/10/1925	FL1	H	Everton	W	7–3
4/2/1931	FL1	H	Blackburn Rovers	W	8–2
5/12/1908	FL1	A	Newcastle United	W	9–1
17/10/1936	FL1	A	Middlesbrough	D	5–5
27/2/1937	FL1	A	WBA	L	4–6
3/9/1955	FL1	A	Blackpool	L	3–7
19/11/1955	FL1	A	Luton Town	L	2–8
29/8/1953	FL1	H	Manchester City	L	4–5
28/12/1935	FL1	H	Arsenal	W	5–4
1/1/1894	FL1	H	Preston NE	W	6–3
12/1/1901	FL1	H	Wolverhampton W	W	7–2
10/3/1906	FL1	H	Wolverhampton W	W	7–2
7/3/1908	FL1	H	Nottingham Forest	W	7–2
21/9/1935	FL1	H	Blackburn Rovers	W	7–2
7/12/1935	FL1	H	Bolton Wanderers	W	7–2
9/12/1961	FL2	H	Swansea Town	W	7–2
22/10/1892	FL1	H	WBA	W	8–1
1/9/1956	FL1	H	Charlton Athletic	W	8–1
13/4/1936	FL1	A	Birmingham	W	7–2
30/1/1915	FL1	A	Oldham Athletic	W	5–4
25/12/1926	FL1	A	Everton	L	4–5
28/11/1903	FL1	A	Derby County	L	2–7
1/11/1930	FL1	A	Sheffield Wednesday	L	2–7
22/3/1909	FL1	A	Blackburn Rovers	L	1–8

BORE DRAWS

Sunderland have been involved in 287 no-score draws in league competition. Stoke City and Middlesbrough are our most boring opponents with 11 goalless league games each.

NARROW WINS

Sunderland have won 330 league games 1–0 and lost 198 games 1–0.

ALL SQUARE

459 league games involving Sunderland have ended 1–1; 219 away and 240 at home. Sunderland's highest score draws are as follows:

19/1/1907	FL1	H	Liverpool	D	5–5
17/10/1936	FL1	A	Middlesbrough	D	5–5
2/1/1895	FL1	H	Aston Villa	D	4–4
22/12/1928	FL1	H	Sheffield United	D	4–4
12/11/1955	FL1	H	Burnley	D	4–4

THE 92 CLUB

Sunderland have scored 5 goals in a league match 92 times; 28 away from home and 64 times on Wearside.

INCREDIBLE FEAT

In the two seasons 1891/92 and 1892/93 combined, Sunderland played 117 league, cup and friendly games. They lost just 18 of those and scored a mammoth 416 goals!

THE GAME OF THREE HALVES

On 1 September 1894 Sunderland entertained Derby County. The record books show that Sunderland won 8–0 with Johnny Campbell scoring a hat-trick; however, those facts mask a very bizarre game.

Due to the original referee for the game having been delayed at York station (he missed his connection), the game commenced with a deputy officiating. At half time the score was 3–0 to Sunderland.

The original referee then turned up and much to the amazement of players, officials and spectators he started the game again! The 'second half' saw Sunderland race into another 3–0 lead and by the end of the 'third half' (*sic*) they had scored 11 goals that afternoon, notching another 5 in that final period.

The match is remembered as 'The Game of Three Halves'. Technically Sunderland won 11–0. Amazing but true.

MILESTONE GAMES

1,000th league game	v Oldham Athletic	0–0	17/2/1923
2,000th league game	v Burnley	1–5	5/12/1953
3,000th league game	v Mansfield Town	2–1	22/10/1977
4,000th league game	v Leeds United	0–2	16/12/2000

OFF!

The first Sunderland player ever to be ordered from the field of play in a competitive match was Hugh Wilson on 14 September 1896 in a league game at Stoke City. The home side were awarded a controversial penalty by the referee, Mr Kingscott of Derby, and he had great trouble in getting the Sunderland players to stop encroaching as the kick was about to be taken. Eventually Hyslop scored from the spot kick but Wilson was far from happy and continued to back chat the referee. The official was left with no choice but to order the Sunderland player off.

What has never been recorded before is that the first Sunderland player to be sent off in any game was probably during the 1–1 home friendly match against Wolves on 18 February 1890. There was an incident in the goalmouth between Rose of Wolves and Smith of Sunderland; the referee immediately stopped the game. A long argument followed between Mr Douglas, the umpires and players from both sides which ended with Smith and Rose being ordered from the field. It was said that Smith had charged the goalkeeper who retaliated by seizing Smith around the throat and a short struggle followed. Half time was called immediately. During the interval both players approached the referee to apologise for their behaviour but were not allowed to return.

Wolves refused to return to the pitch after half time unless their man was reinstated but the referee refused and the teams were left with 10 men a side with Wykes going into goal for Wolves.

POLICE PROTECTION

On 18 December 1886, Sunderland travelled to play Birtley in the Durham County Cup. A bruising encounter saw Sunderland win 2–1, the winner being an own goal. At the end of the game the Sunderland team had to be escorted from the field by two policemen as the crowd reacted with hostility to the home side's defeat.

A LIABILITY

At the end of the 1895/96 season, an important development took place. Sunderland AFC were converted into a limited liability company with a share capital of £5,000.

GOALIE SCORES GOAL

On 14 April 1900 Sunderland defeated Manchester City 3–1 at Roker Park. However, the talking point wasn't the victory.

A handball in the penalty area by a visiting defender resulted in a penalty kick to the home side. Sunderland's Ferguson was obliged to take the kick three times due to defenders' 'over anxiety to resume operations.' His third attempt struck the goalkeeper and rebounded to Jones who cleared easily. This was considered very unfair on Sunderland as Ferguson had converted twice only to be made to retake the kick because of encroachment by the City defenders.

However, what happened subsequently was even more extraordinary. From Sunderland's next attack, which ended in the ball going out of play, the resulting goal kick was booted upfield by the City goalkeeper, Williams, where it was caught by the strong wind and carried right into the home goalmouth. The Sunderland goalkeeper Doig was deceived by the flight and somehow managed to get an ineffective touch to the ball which travelled on into the net!

Manchester City had equalised!

THEY SAID IT ...

'Amid all the hype and hysteria, it might have gone unnoticed that Sunderland are up too, but this will be put to right once Roker's red-and-white hordes begin their travels through the Premiership. Contrary to popular myth, the Geordies of Newcastle are not the most fanatically exuberant followers in British football; that honour belongs to their Sunderland rivals, the Mackems. Whether disdaining the option of sitting down for the entire duration of matches, standing bare-chested throughout the coldest January afternoon (I'm talking male fans here – Wearsiders are not that exuberant), or collectively ignoring the evidence of their eyes and acclaiming their team as the greatest the world has ever seen, Sunderland followers are in a class of their own.'

Paul Wilson, a journalist with the *Observer* in his Sportsview section, previewing the 1996/97 Premiership season

'The supporters are the football club. It's their football club and I'm just the manager of it. And when I'm dead and gone the supporters will still be here. I know it sounds crap, but that's the way it is.'

Peter Reid on the Sunderland supporters

CELEBRITY RED & WHITES

Over the years there have been many famous names that have been linked with supporting Sunderland, some proven and some not:

Steve Cram	Olympic athlete
Alf Wight aka James Herriot	British vet and writer
Frank Bough	television presenter
Sir Tim Rice	musical producer
Kate Adie	news reporter
Louise Taylor	journalist (*The Times*)
Dave Stewart	pop star (Eurythmics)
Neil Tennant	pop star (Pet Shop Boys)
Brian Marwood	footballer/television presenter
Paul Collingwood	England cricketer
Heather Mills	model
Martin O'Neill	football manager
Peter O'Toole	actor
Padraig Harrington	golfer
Don Airey	musician (Black Sabbath)
Tasmin Archer	musician
Eric Idle	comedian
Billy Hardy	boxer
Mark Webber	Formula 1 racing driver

For some, there are obvious reasons why they support the Black Cats – i.e. they were born in the city. For others the link is not so obvious. Sir Tim Rice was taken to watch Arsenal by his father, but rather than going away with a love of all things Highbury he came away transfixed by the red and white striped Sunderland shirts. Peter O'Toole was allegedly related through marriage to Ernie Taylor who played for Sunderland in the 1950s.

THEY SAID IT ...

'I had never known so much money. I walked through the streets with the notes clutched tightly in my hand and went into a cinema for the matinee to celebrate the momentous occasion, still holding onto the money like grim death.'

Raich Carter describes his panic on being given his £10 signing-on fee for Sunderland in 1931

THEY SAID IT ...

'I was Sunderland crazy as a kid. They were the only team for me.'

Ralph Coates, Burnley, Tottenham Hotspur and England forward

BOTTLING IT

On 28 December 1920 thirty-one-year-old Owen Coggins appeared before Sunderland Magistrates accused of hitting a fellow Sunderland supporter with a bottle in the Roker End during the Boxing Day encounter with Bolton Wanderers. In his defence Coggins indicated that previously he had himself been hit over the head with an axe that had left him incapable with the smallest amount of alcohol. He admitted he had been to a party on the day of the match, making his way to Roker Park by taxi cab. He was fined £5 by local magistrates and ordered to pay £2 in compensation to his unfortunate fellow Sunderland fan who had been bottled!

SUNDERLAND'S FINE BUILDINGS

Following a decision to build Sunderland AFC a new football stadium, local architects and brothers William and Thomas Ridley Milburn were responsible for drawing up the plans. The brothers had been responsible for designing Sunderland's Law Courts, fire station and Empire Theatre. The new ground was to be named Roker Park.

DEATH HITS CELTIC

On 18 January 1928, Sunderland Reserves defeated Walker Celtic 11–0 at Roker Park. Billy Death scored 7 of the home side's goals, including a 4-minute hat-trick. The score at half time was 0–0!

NO ENGLISH PLEASE, WE'RE SUNDERLAND

When Alan Brown was appointed manager of Sunderland AFC in July 1957 he was Sunderland AFC's very first permanent English manager. Until that date the previous incumbents were either Scottish or, in the case of Bob Kyle, Irish.

WARM PLAYERS

On 29 October 1907, Stewarts the Tailors, who operated from a shop in High Street West in Sunderland, offered a free overcoat to any Sunderland player who scored two goals in a match during the months of November and December. Sam Raybould was the first player to win an overcoat; just four days later, when he scored two in the 4–0 win over Chelsea at Roker Park!

RARE PENALTY MISS

One of the best penalty-takers in the history of Sunderland AFC was Seaham-born striker Gary Rowell. He missed only two spot kicks in his first team career. One was against Leyton Orient and the other came in a friendly against the Australian Federation on 15 November 1976. The Aussie goalkeeper Clarke saved the effort.

NOW WE KNOW WHO YOU ARE

On 17 October 1993, Sunderland lost 4–1 at Middlesbrough in a league match. While a Sunderland defeat isn't one for the record books, the game was ground-breaking in that it was the first time that the Sunderland players had worn squad numbers and their names on the back of the shirts. For the record, number 1 was worn by Alec Chamberlain.

TOP 10 SUNDERLAND GOALSCORERS

Name	League	FA Cup	League Cup	Other	Total
Bobby Gurney	205	23	0	0	228
Charlie Buchan	209	13	0	0	222
David Halliday	156	9	0	0	165
George Holley	151	9	0	0	160
Johnny Campbell	136	18	0	0	154
Kevin Phillips	113	10	5	2	130
Raich Carter	118	9	0	1	128
Jimmy Millar	107	19	0	2	128
Arthur Bridgett	108	8	0	0	116
Patsy Gallagher	100	7	0	0	107

THEY SAID IT ...

'I would have died for Alan Brown.'

1973 FA Cup winner Micky Horswill's verdict on his first manager at Sunderland and the impact he had on his career

THE GYPSY'S CURSE

On 27 February 1892, Sunderland's James Hannah was walking along Newcastle Road having called into the football club's headquarters in Ellerslie Terrace to find out whether he was in the team for Saturday.

As fate would have it he bumped into a gypsy caravan. The driver of the first carriage shouted out that Sunderland would lose the forthcoming cup tie. Hannah was then introduced to the driver's wife and as she held his hand in a vice like grip she said to him that 'Sunderland would never win the English Cup until a Scotch (*sic*) lady becomes Queen of England.'

Sunderland won the FA Cup for the first time in the club's history in 1937. The trophy was presented to club captain Raich Carter by Queen Elizabeth, daughter of Scottish landowner the Earl of Strathmore, who had ascended the throne with her husband following the shock abdication of Edward VIII in December 1936. Strange but true!

SHOPPED

In the late 1940s Sunderland player Willie Watson owned a sports shop on Newcastle Road in Sunderland. Not to be outdone, Len Shackleton opened one a few years later on New Durham Road. However, they weren't the first Sunderland players to go into business in the Town. The likes of Charlie Buchan had owned a sports outfitter with his friend A. Lowings at Blandford Street as far back as 1924.

TURNCOATS?

It was reported by the *Sunderland Echo* that some 500 Sunderland supporters made the trip to Wembley in 1932 to cheer on their arch-rivals Newcastle United in that years FA Cup Final. One of the Sunderland supporters was spotted carrying a lucky Black Cat into the ground. The Magpies defeated Arsenal 2–1.

THEY SAID IT ...

'No club could get nor wish for a better one.'
Sunderland chairman Fred Taylor, presenting trainer Billy Williams with his long service award in May 1929. Williams had been with the club for thirty-two years

'There was so many people trying to get in they knocked the big gates down and although the official attendance was 45,000 I think there was more like 80,000 inside.'
Bobby Charlton the Manchester United legend commenting on the chaos that ensued before the 1964 Roker Park FA Cup tie involving the Red Devils

'Why there's a tyre running past us!'
**A Sunderland supporter on his way to the 1919
Roker Park clash with Newcastle United when his taxi cab
broke down**

'To fight in this war would be a denial of my faith and belief
in the Fatherhood of God as revealed in the teaching of Jesus
Christ.'
**Sunderland Reserve forward Norman Gaudie appearing
before a military tribunal in 1916 explaining his refusal to
fight in the First World War**

'It brought her to alright, but the orange juice and her, err,
complexion made a rare mess. That was the last of my orange!'
**A Sunderland supporter at the 1933 club record attendance
game versus Derby County at Roker Park, with his novel
method of bringing round a female supporter who had fainted
– he squeezed orange juice onto her face!**

'I wonder how much Gladwin got for putting the ball through
his own goal?'
**The last sarcastic words spoken by a Newcastle fan,
with Sunderland's giant defender within earshot, just before
he hit the ground following a collision with Charlie's fist
in 1913**

'We thought nothing of walking the five miles each way, then
standing on the terraces for the game.'
**MP Willie Hamilton, born in Herrington, recounting his early
trips to Roker Park in his 1992 autobiography
*Blood on the Walls***

ROLL UP, ROLL UP

It's doubtful that the clubs record attendance will ever
be topped and even more pertinent is whether any of the
following highest crowds to watch Sunderland on Wearside
will be beaten.

75,118	v Derby County	FA Cup 6th round (r)	8/3/33
68,004	v Newcastle United	Football League 1	4/3/50
66,654	v Newcastle United	Football League 1	9/10/54
65,125	v Norwich City	FA Cup 5th round	10/2/51
64,888	v Blackpool	Football League 1	8/10/49
64,436	v Arsenal	Football League 1	18/9/48
63,251	v Manchester United	Football League 1	18/2/50
63,016	v Sheffield United	FA Cup 5th round	14/2/31
62,817	v Everton	FA Cup 5th round	15/2/64
62,487	v Middlesbrough	Football League 1	7/4/50
62,420	v Newcastle United	Football League 1	2/3/63
62,413	v Derby County	Football League 1	21/1/50

The record attendances for a floodlit game on Wearside are:

| 58,527 | v Southampton | FA Cup 3rd round (r) | 10/1/62 |
| 55,436 | v Dynamo Moscow | Friendly | 14/10/55 |

SICK OF SUNDERLAND

You had to feel for Wolverhampton Wanderers during the 1936/37 season. Sunderland met them five times in the space of 22 days and the Midlands team never won a solitary game. Three of the matches were in the FA Cup that the Black Cats went on to win in that campaign.

YOU'VE GOT TO PICK A POCKET OR TWO

At Roker Park on 28 August 1937, two Tynesiders were arrested in the Fulwell End by police for 'frequenting the place with intent to pick-pocket.' Their tactic was for one to jostle a fan, and while he was preoccupied, the other one stole his wallet. One Sunderland fan complained that he had lost a 10-shilling note. The two men, one from Newcastle and the other from Gateshead, were found guilty six weeks later. One was sentenced to four months' hard labour and the other to six months.

REFUSED TO PLAY

Although not a league club until 1890, Sunderland were still eligible to play in the FA Cup. The club was proceeding very nicely in the 1888/89 version with a win over Elswick Rangers and a defeat of Newcastle East End. However, when drawn to play local rivals Sunderland Albion in the next round Sunderland promptly refused and were scratched from the competition. The reason was simple; they didn't want Albion to prosper financially from the large gate that the match would attract as they may have become a threat to Sunderland.

WALKED TO NEWCASTLE

In the 1908/09 season, Sunderland not only defeated Newcastle at St James' Park 9–1 but also met them in the FA Cup at the same venue. Thousands of Sunderland fans made the journey to Newcastle, mainly by trains that left the town centre every few minutes. However, four hundred men who could not afford the train fare walked from Sunderland to Newcastle. Their reward was a 2–2 draw.

As a postscript; at the replay 1,000 supporters charged the gates at the Fulwell End with 300 gaining free admittance before police, with truncheons drawn, restored order.

DIVINE INTERVENTION?

In the early years of Sunderland AFC the club relied heavily on 'Scotchmen' to fill the team. However, Wearside sorties north of the border were not welcome due to the English pinching all of the Scottish footballing talent. In order to hide their true motives, Sunderland officials Tom Watson and Samuel Tyzack used to dress as clergymen.

As a result of such raids, Sunderland AFC became known in Scotland as 'the Barbary Coasters'!

THEY SAID IT ...

'I complained to the referee after only five minutes that I had been punched in the ribs by John Fashanu but he told me to just get on with the game.'
Sunderland striker Thomas Hauser commenting on his rough treatment by the Crazy Gang

'Sunderland lost more leads this season than Inspector Clouseau.'
David Lacey, a journalist with the *Guardian*, commenting on Sunderland's profligacy during the 1990/91 season

'Unbelievable. How can you be relegated and have people chanting for you like that? Grown men out there are crying; they hurt as much as the players. It's difficult to put my feelings into words.'
Sunderland manager Denis Smith reacting to the sights and sounds at Maine Road following the Black Cats' last-gasp 1990/91 relegation

'If points were awarded for class from the terraces instead of on the pitch, Sunderland would have few worries about First Division survival. Sadly, they are not, and despite the presence of the most numerous, boisterous and insanely optimistic travelling support in the league, the Wearsiders will return to the Second Division whence they came. But even in bidding farewell to the First Division the Sunderland fans could not resist one more rousing chorus of "by far the greatest team the world has ever seen" in flagrant disregard of the empirical evidence. The First Division can only be the poorer for lack of such traditional support.'
Paul Wilson, a journalist with the *Observer*, commenting on Sunderland's 1990/91 relegation at Maine Road

'There was one occasion in the first half when four Wednesday defenders tried to hit Gurney.'
The *Sunderland Echo*'s take on Sheffield Wednesday's novel tactics to stop Sunderland's ace marksman Bobby Gurney from scoring in the first game of the 1936/37 season

'Sunderland were a shambles, their defending lacking only the presence of Brian Rix and a bit of trouser dropping to make the farce complete.'

The *Sunday Times* reporting of the debacle at Meadow Lane on 9 March 1993

NICKNAMES

John Kay, aka **The Red & White Tractor**: John Kay was a Sunderland full-back from 1987 to 1996. His no-nonsense style endeared him to the Roker Park faithful. In a game against Leeds United, John Kay 'tackled' the ex-Newcastle United player Peter Haddock. The Yorkshire side's manager at the time, Howard Wilkinson, likened the injury sustained to his player in the '50-50' challenge to having 'been run over by a tractor.'

Martin Smith, aka **Son of Pelé**: Forward Martin Smith was a local lad who signed associate schoolboy forms with Sunderland in 1988. He stayed with the club for eleven years. At a time when there was a dearth of talent on display at Roker Park, Smith was at times the only bright spot on some otherwise very bleak Wearside footballing days. For some sublime skill in a red and white shirt he was nicknamed 'Son of Pelé'.

THEY SAID IT ...

' . . . to be honest that season was pretty much a piece of piss.'
John Kay's frank assessment of Sunderland's difficulty in obtaining promotion from the old Third Division in 1987/88

STRANGE BUT TRUE

Billy Hughes swapped his 1973 FA Cup-winning strip for a gold record by the Scottish pop group Sweet.

THEY SAID IT …

'He knocked it past me once, but fortunately as he was running past to get it, he ran into my elbow.'

Former Sunderland full back Joe Bolton on his 'accidental' collision with John Chiedozie of Notts County in the mid-1970s

SUNDERLAND SONGS

'Who needs Cantona when we've got Dicky Ord?'

Ironic song from the Sunderland faithful in homage to defender Richard Ord, at a time when Eric Cantona was one of the best players in the world for Manchester United

'Sit down Pinocchio, Sit down Pinocchio!'

First heard at Anfield when Sunderland visited for a league encounter. Phil Thompson was the then Liverpool manager

Over sea and over shore
You'll always hear the Roker Roar
The name will echo round the land
The name of our team, Sunderland
Sunderland will never die
We'll keep the red flag flying high

Sunderland our pride and joy
Jim Baxter is our darling boy
We'll follow them through thick and thin
And cheer them on until they win
Sunderland need never fear
We'll keep the red flag flying here

Chant from Sunderland fans in the 1960s to the tune of 'The Red Flag'

CUP TRIVIA

The first recorded occasion when the FA Cup and the Scottish equivalent were on the same pitch together was on 6 October 1937 when Sunderland took on Glasgow Celtic at Roker Park in a friendly match.

The very first time that the Scottish Cup was paraded on English soil was when Renton visited Sunderland in 1888. The trophy was put on display at Havelock House, a large drapery store, for the duration of Renton's stay in the town.

ABANDONED GAMES

In the 130-year history of Sunderland football club there have only ever been six abandoned games.

1/9/1894	FL	Sunderland 3–0 Derby County
		Game of three halves – restarted

10/1/1903	FL	Liverpool 2–2 Sunderland
		Bad light and heavy rain

5/2/1913	FAC	Manchester City 0–2 Sunderland
		Improper fan behaviour

1/1/1985	FL	Sunderland 0–0 Liverpool
		Dangerous pitch – icebound

12/12/1993	FL	Grimsby 0–0 Sunderland
		Waterlogged pitch

8/4/2006	PL	Sunderland 0–1 Fulham
		Waterlogged pitch

HOW MANY PLAYERS?

The number of players used by Sunderland in each of their English League Championship victories was as follows:

1891/92	15
1892/93	15
1894/95	18
1901/02	19
1912/13	22
1935/36	23

SUNDERLAND FIRSTS

First FA Cup tie: 1884/85 v Redcar – lost 3–1

First league match: 1890/91 v Burnley – lost 3–2

First league cup tie: 1960/61 v Brentford – lost 4–3

First match in Europe: 1973/74 v Vasas Budapest – won 2–0

First Anglo-Italian Cup match: 1969/70 v Lazio – won 3–1

THOMAS HEMY AND THE HEMY PAINTING

Anyone walking into the main foyer of the Stadium of Light can't help notice the stunning painting, behind its protective glass casing, of the 1895 fixture between Sunderland and Aston Villa played at the then home ground of Newcastle Road. That the match ended 4–4 was fairly inconsequential; that the painting is perhaps the oldest of an Association Football match in the world, isn't.

The 'Hemy Painting' as it is commonly referred to is in recognition of the artist Thomas Maria Madawaska Hemy. In celebration of Sunderland AFC's third English league championship, in 1894/95, the football club commissioned

Hemy, a local artist who resided in Sunderland, to paint a picture of the team in action and the game against Villa was the match chosen. The painting has over the years had two titles; 'A Corner Kick' and 'The Last Minute – Now or Never'.

Thomas Marie Madawaska Hemy was born in 1852 off the Murtar Var Rocks near the Brazilian Coast in 1852. The 'Marie' was in due deference to the Catholic Church of which his father was a devout member and the 'Madawaska' in homage to the ship that he was born on. The ship *Madawaska* was registered in Canada and named after a river in Ontario. His sea birth was owing to the family emigrating (temporarily) to Australia, leaving Liverpool in 1852, bound for Sydney Harbour.

The family's roots were in Newcastle, where Charles (Thomas's brother) had been born, and having found life tough in Melbourne, where they had settled, the family returned to the north-east in 1854. At aged fourteen, Thomas Hemy ran away to sea for four years sailing exotic seas such as The Dardanelles aboard such ships as *The Brindisi*, a passage of his life that he recounted in his autobiography *Deep Sea Days*.

It is perhaps then no coincidence, given all of this, that Hemy's brother (Thomas had nine brothers and three sisters) Charles Napier Hemy would become one of the finest British maritime painters to have lived, a talent that was to be passed on to Thomas. All the family had a love of the sea and the Arts; Hemy's Father Henri was an accomplished musician.

Back in England a substantial amount of Thomas's time was spent at the mouth of the Tyne River painting boats or inspiring paintings of shipwrecks, perhaps his most famous work being 'The Wreck of the Birkenhead'. However, he also gave us masterpieces such as 'The Eton Wall Game' and of course 'The Last Minute – Now Or Never'.

However, it would be wrong to think of Hemy as a parochial north-east painter. We have read about his sailing exploits which gave him a very broad horizon and he also exhibited at such places as The Royal Academy in London and studied at the Antwerp Academy of Arts for two years, working under Charles Verlat.

He was often commissioned to paint and had his subsequent efforts purchased by such people as Lord Charles Beresford. Towards the end of his life Hemy left the north-east and settled in St Helens on the Isle Of Wight where he died on an unknown date in 1937.

THE McCOMBIE AFFAIR

In the close season of 1903/04 Sunderland AFC gave one of their players, Andrew McCombie, £100 to enable him to start up in business. It was given on the understanding that, on receiving a benefit game, he would repay the money. Everything came into the public arena in January 1904 when McCombie refused to pay the money back saying that the £100 had been a gift.

The Football Association made an enquiry into the £100 'gift' and ordered Sunderland to take legal action against McCombie. However, a court of law judged that the money constituted a loan. The FA took exception to this ruling and agreed with McCombie that it had been a 're-signing/win/draw bonus', violating the games rules. The books were deemed as not showing a true record of the clubs financial affairs.

The upshot was that Sunderland AFC were fined £250 and six directors were suspended for two-and-a-half years, Alex Watson for eighteen months and Alex Mackie for three months.

McCombie was transfer-listed by the club and there was an instant clamour for his signature as he was one of the best footballers of his time. He could have gone anywhere, but his desire to stay in the North-East swayed his decision. McCombie subsequently signed for Newcastle United with the Magpies paying a world record £700 for his signature. To put McCombie's playing prowess into perspective, the next season, his first for the Magpies, would see the black and whites crowned league champions. McCombie was only twenty-eight years old and had the footballing world at his feet.

14 MOST DRAMATIC LAST GAMES
OF THE SEASON

1896/97 – 26 April 1897 – Sunderland 2–0 Newton Heath
Sunderland's poorest league season to that date saw the Black
Cats compete in an end of season series of Test Matches to
retain their First Division place. They needed to defeat Newton
Heath on the very last match and did so, 2–0, at Newcastle
Road.

1902/03 – 25 April 1903 – Newcastle United 1–0 Sunderland
Sunderland travelled to St James' Park, the home of their bitter
rivals, needing a win to clinch the league title, with Aston Villa
and Sheffield Wednesday breathing down their necks. A 1–0
defeat for Sunderland meant they ended the season in third
place, just one point from an elusive championship.

1949/50 – 6 May 1950 – Sunderland 4–1 Chelsea
With Wolves and Portsmouth just 1 point ahead of Sunderland
in third place, the Black Cats would be league champions if
they won and the other two lost. Sunderland kept their end
of the bargain by hammering Chelsea; alas both Wolves and
Portsmouth won too.

1957/58 – 26 April 1958 – Portsmouth 0–2 Sunderland
Sunderland travelled to Fratton Park knowing that only a
win could save them from their very first relegation. Despite
winning with two goals from Don Kitchenbrand, their
closest rivals, Leicester City, also won, at Birmingham City,
so demoting the Black Cats to the Second Division after an
unbroken sixty-eight years in the top flight.

1961/62 – 28 April 1962 – Swansea Town 1–1 Sunderland
Sunderland were looking for an away win to guarantee them
a first promotion back to the top flight with Leyton Orient
breathing down their necks. The Welsh side were near the foot
of the table. Alas it wasn't to be as the red and white could
only muster a draw which saw the London side promoted
along with Liverpool.

1962/63 – 18 May 1963 – Sunderland 0–1 Chelsea
The Wearsiders took the field for their final match of the season knowing that a draw against Chelsea, who lay third, would be enough too see them promoted. Sunderland lost at Roker Park in front of nearly 50,000 and were pipped to the two promotion places by the Londoners, on goal difference, and Stoke City.

1969/70 – 15 April 1970 – Sunderland 0–1 Liverpool
Fighting for their First Division lives, Sunderland entered the final day of the season knowing that a home win over fifth placed Liverpool would see them leapfrog Crystal Palace to safety. They lost and went down.

1976/77 – 19 May 1977 – Everton 2–0 Sunderland
With Stoke City and Spurs already relegated, Sunderland travelled to Goodison Park knowing that a draw would be good enough to keep them up; they could even afford to lose if there was a winner from the Coventry City v. Bristol City game played the same night. The latter two teams lay below Sunderland in the table. In a dramatic twist of fate, Sunderland lost and with that news filtering through to Highfield Road, the two City's played out a tame draw to ensure their survival.

1979/80 – 12 May 1980 – Sunderland 2–0 West Ham United
With Leicester already promoted, FA Cup winners West Ham United travelled north to Roker Park as Sunderland aimed for the win that would see them leapfrog Birmingham City and Chelsea into an automatic promotion place on the very last Second Division fixture of the season. In front of 47,000 Sunderland won with goals from Arnott and Cummins to seal a place back in the top flight.

1986/87 – 17 May 1987 – Sunderland 4–3 Gillingham
Having snatched defeat from the jaws of victory against Barnsley at Roker Park, the play-offs saw Sunderland play Kent club Gillingham. Lose over two legs and Sunderland would play Third Division football for the first time in their history. Sunderland lost the first leg 2–1 and in typical style won 4–3 in the second leg, but were relegated on the away goals rule. Trust Sunderland!

1989/90 – 28 May 1990 – Sunderland 0–1 Swindon Town
Having finished the Division Two league season in sixth place, Sunderland defeated arch-rivals Newcastle United over two legs to take a well-earned place in a Wembley play-off final. Backed predictably by 70 per cent of the crowd, and in true style, Sunderland lost. However, an inquiry into Swindon's financial affairs saw them stripped of a victory and Sunderland were promoted in bizarre fashion. This could only happen to Sunderland!

1990/91 – 11 May 1991 – Manchester City 3–2 Sunderland
Backed by 15,000 supporters at Maine Road, Sunderland had to win and hope Luton Town didn't do likewise to secure their First Division status. Predictably, Sunderland lost and Luton won!

1996/97 – 11 May 1997 – Wimbledon 1–0 Sunderland
Backed by another 15,000 fans, the Black Cats made the long trip to South London to take on Wimbledon at Selhurst Park, knowing that with three clubs below them in the league table a draw would likely be enough to see them safe from the drop. Unfortunately the theory was a better prospect than the practice as Sunderland lost against a reluctant Wimbledon side, while Coventry City won at Tottenham to send the red and whites down yet again.

1997/98 – 25 May 1998 – Charlton Athletic 4–4 Sunderland
Following a superb home win over Sheffield United in the play-offs at the club's new Stadium of Light, the Black Cats travelled to Wembley to take on a Charlton side that included locally raised Sunderland fan Clive Mendonca in their lineup. In what was widely regarded as one of the best games ever seen at Wembley Stadium the game see-sawed until even hat-trick hero Mendonca couldn't separate the sides. In a dramatic penalty shoot-out, it was inevitably (and predictably) a Sunderland player who missed and the red and whites this time succumbed to a 7–6 thriller of a shoot-out.

2008/09 – 24 May 2009 – Sunderland 2–3 Chelsea
Sunderland went into the match knowing that only a strange set of results would send them down. Arch-rivals Newcastle

United, third bottom, had to win to catch us up; meanwhile Hull (fourth bottom) could stay up at our expense if they drew at home to Premier League Champions Manchester United and Sunderland lost heavily to Chelsea. It was yet another nervous week for followers of Sunderland AFC. In the end it didn't matter that Sunderland lost 3–2 as the three teams below them also lost, including arch-rivals Newcastle United who were relegated to the second tier of English football for the first time in twenty years; cue celebrations on Wearside!

SUNDERLAND MILESTONES

1879   Sunderland AFC formed in Hendon, a district of the then town, by James Allan as Sunderland & District Teachers' Association.

1880   The club is opened to all professions, not exclusively teachers, and the name changed to Sunderland Association Football Club. First recorded game played by the club at home to Ferryhill.

1882   Sunderland AFC move from The Blue House Field to a new ground at Groves Field.

1883   Sunderland AFC move again, this time to the Clay Dolly Field at Horatio Street.

1884   Sunderland AFC take up residency at Abbs Field, Fulwell. There they defeat Castletown 23–0 to record the club's highest ever win. Club founder James Allan scores 12.

1885   Sunderland AFC award their very first testimonial, for full-back Watson who had sustained a compound fracture of the leg in a previous game.

1886   Sunderland move to Newcastle Road, where they would remain for twelve years.

1887   The famous red and white striped shirts are revealed
        on 24 September for the match with Darlington
        St Augustine's.

1888   Club founder James Allan voted off the Committee.
        He forms Sunderland Albion.

1890   Sunderland elected to play in the Football League,
        replacing Stoke City. They lose their first league match
        3–2 at home to Burnley. The 7–2 defeat of Aston
        Villa, which paved the way for Sunderland's elevated
        status, saw McGregor the Villa Director indicate that
        'Sunderland had a talented man in every position.'
        Team Of All The Talents legend born.

1892   Sunderland crowned Football League champions for
        the first time following a 6–1 defeat of Blackburn
        Rovers. Sunderland also defeat Aston Villa 6–1 in
        Birmingham. Possible that this is the Team Of All The
        Talents game. Sunderland Albion go bust.

1893   Sunderland retain their league crown and in doing so
        become the first team to score 100 goals in a league
        season.

1894   'Game of three halves' against Derby County.

1895   Sunderland AFC win their third league title.
        Sunderland 4–4 Aston Villa becomes the subject for
        'The Hemy Painting'. Sunderland defeat Fairfield
        11–1 in the English Cup. Sunderland become 'World
        Champions' defeating Heart of Midlothian in
        Edinburgh.

1896   On 12 August Sunderland AFC become a limited
        liability company.

1898   Sunderland take up residence at Roker Park.
        They defeat Liverpool in the first game at the new
        stadium.

1902   League championship returns to Wearside for the
       fourth time.

1903   Sunderland win the Sheriff Of London Shield, the
       forerunner of the Charity Shield.

1904   Sunderland rocked by the McCombie scandal.

1905   Bob Kyle becomes manager of Sunderland AFC.

1908   Sunderland thrash arch-rivals Newcastle United 9–1 at
       St James' Park.

1911   Sunderland sign Charlie Buchan.

1913   Sunderland become league champions for the fifth
       time. Narrowly miss out on the double losing the FA
       Cup Final 1–0 to Aston Villa at The Crystal Palace.

1928   Johnny Cochrane replaces Kyle in the managerial hot
       seat, joining from St Mirren.

1931   Sunderland reach the FA Cup semi-final, but lose to
       Birmingham at Elland Road.

1936   Sunderland become league champions for the sixth
       time. Goalkeeper Jimmy Thorpe tragically dies
       following the home game against Chelsea. Sunderland
       defeat Arsenal to take the Charity Shield.

1937   Sunderland wins the FA Cup for the first time in the
       club's history, defeating Preston North End 3–1 at
       Wembley Stadium.

1942   Sunderland loses the War Cup Final to Wolverhampton
       Wanderers.

1949   Non-league Yeovil Town knock Sunderland out of the
       FA Cup.

1957   Sunderland is rocked by an illegal payments scandal that would see players and officials initially banned *sine die* from football in England.

1958   Sunderland relegated to the Second Division for the first time in their history despite winning the final game of the season at Portsmouth.

1964   Sunderland promoted from the Second Division.

1966   Sunderland host World Cup matches at Roker Park.

1967   Sunderland franchised and play as the Vancouver Royal Canadians in a close-season North American league.

1970   Sunderland suffers relegation once again.

1973   Sunderland wins the FA Cup against all the odds, defeating Leeds United 1–0 at Wembley Stadium. Ian Porterfield scores the only goal of the game.

1976   Sunderland become Second Division champions for the first time and are promoted back to the First Division.

1977   After just one season back in the top flight, Sunderland are once more relegated.

1980   Sunderland AFC gain promotions after a last day win at home to FA Cup winners West Ham United.

1985   Sunderland perform an unwanted double, losing the Milk Cup final to Norwich City and being relegated in the same season.

1987   Dark days for Sunderland as they are relegated to the Third Division for the first time in their history after an away goals play-off defeat by Gillingham.

1988   Sunderland takes the Third Division by storm, winning it at a canter. Promotion is sealed at Port Vale.

1990 Promoted via the play-offs, despite losing the final to
      Swindon Town.

1991 Sunderland relegated on the last day of the season
      despite the presence of 15,000 fans roaring them on at
      Maine Road.

1992 Sunderland reaches the FA Cup Final where they lose
      to Liverpool 2–0.

1996 Sunderland wins the First Division under manager
      Peter Reid.

1997 Last game at Roker Park. Sunderland relegated on the
      last day of the season, losing to Wimbledon at Selhurst
      Park, despite, once more, being backed by 15,000
      fans, this time in South London. First game at the new
      Stadium of Light.

1998 Sunderland loses on penalties at Wembley Stadium to
      Charlton Athletic in one of the best games ever seen at
      the famous ground.

1999 Sunderland storm to promotion with a record
      105 points.

2000 Sunderland finish seventh in the top flight, their highest
      league placing since 1954/55.

2003 Relegated for the eighth time, with just 19 points.

2005 Football League champions – promoted once more.

2006 Relegated again, this time with just 15 points.
      Chairman Bob Murray sells the club to the Drumaville
      consortium, headed up by ex-player Niall Quinn. Roy
      Keane appointed as manager.

2007 Sunderland promoted again, at the first attempt,
      thrashing Luton at Kenilworth Road to seal the title.

2009   Manager Roy Keane resigns; Ricky Sbragia takes over
        and guides SAFC to Premier League safety, then promptly
        resigns himself. Steve Bruce is handed the reins.

FIRSTS

These are Sunderland's first results in the following competitions:

League:
13 September 1890   v. Burnley (h)   lost 3–2

FA Cup:
8 November 1884   v. Redcar (a)   lost 3–1

League Cup:
26 October 1960   v. Brentford (a)   lost 4–3

European Cup Winners' Cup:
19 September 1973   v. Vasas Budapest (a)   won 2–0

Anglo Italian Cup:
1 May 1969   v. Lazio (h)   won 3–1

Anglo Scottish Cup:
2 august 1975   v. Middlesbrough   lost 3–2

Full Members' Cup:
17 September 1985   v. Grimsby Town (a)   lost 3–2

Freight Rover Trophy:
29 October 1987   v. Scarborough (a)   won 3–0

Simod Cup:
8 November 1988   v. Charlton Athletic (a)   won 1–0

Zenith Data Systems Trophy:
14 November 1989   v. Port Vale (h)   lost 2–1

ILLEGAL PAYMENTS!
THE BIGGEST OWN GOAL IN
FOOTBALL HISTORY

Regulation 59 (a), Maximum Wage, of the Football League, published in its 1938 Jubilee publication, stated that, 'The maximum wage, except as hereinafter provided shall be £5 per week, with annual rises of £1 per week to a maximum of £6 per week during the close season and £8 per week during the close season. A player, whose registration is transferred from one club to another, may be paid the rate of wages he is receiving at the time of transfer.'

In January 1957 a letter, signed by a 'Mr Smith' made allegations about under-the-counter payments by Sunderland AFC. The then Secretary of the Football League opened up an inquiry into the matter. On the verge of giving up on the issue as that of a disgruntled prankster, a final look at the club's accounts revealed a pencil note on the draft accounts asking 'where do I post this?' The figure, for the purchase of straw, amounted to around £3,000. At the time there was no undersoil heating at football grounds and in order to ward off snow and particularly ice, football clubs would cover the pitch with straw in the winter.

Hardaker, the League Secretary immediately telephoned his brother Ernest who was chairman of Hull Rugby League Club and in his autobiography recounted the contents of the conversation:

'How much does it cost to cover your ground with straw in a normal sort of winter?'

'It would depend on how many Saturdays were involved,' Ernest replied.

'Well,' said Hardaker, 'if I gave you £3,000 would you be able to mange for a season?'

'Blow me,' Ernest answered. 'For that we'd manage twenty-five seasons.'

Sunderland's cover was blown wide open and their scam was simple. They had placed orders for both straw and tarmac, far in excess of what was required. When the suppliers came to deliver the items they gave credit notes to SAFC for the amounts returned; in turn SAFC cashed the credit notes in with the suppliers and used the cash to pay their players over and above the permitted maximum wage. In effect under-the-counter payments. It was determined that the practice had been going on for five years and amounted to £5,217.

On 10 April 1957 the Football League made its ruling into the affair. Sunderland were fined £5,000 which was the biggest fine ever issued to a football club. Three of the Directors were barred from football *sine die*, including Ditchburn and the vice-chairman. The rest of the Board were severely censured. Worse was to follow. On 25 April 1957 five Sunderland players were hauled in front of an FA Commission to answer for their part in the scandal, Ray Daniel, Ken Chisholm, Billy Elliott, Willie Fraser and Johnny Hannigan. On the instructions of the PFA lawyers, all five remained silent and in doing so condemned themselves to *sine die* bans.

A long and protracted saga followed and in the end the five players in question admitted to receiving under-the-counter payments. Their *sine die* bans were lifted and lesser sanctions were imposed. However, the damage was done. Bill Murray the Sunderland manager was fined. One month later he resigned, ending a twenty-eight year association with his beloved Sunderland AFC.

The saga still rumbled on for another five years and eventually, in April 1962, with the maximum wage now abolished, the High Court in London ruled that the FA and Football League had no power to act as they did. Sunderland AFC lay in tatters for nothing.

Within one year of the initial suspensions and fines, Sunderland were relegated for the first time in their long and then illustrious history; a club humbled and embarrassed. The heart of an institution had been ripped out.

It was mooted that 'Mr Smith' who made the original allegations was either a disgruntled director or player and it looks, amazingly, as though the club was brought to its knees by an insider; perhaps the biggest own goal in football history.

CHAMPIONS!

Sunderland have been crowned English League Champions six times. Here are the final league tables for each of those seasons:

1891/92

	P	W	D	L	F	A	W	D	L	F	A	Pts
			Home						Away			
Sunderland	26	13	0	0	55	11	8	0	5	38	25	42
Preston NE	26	12	0	1	42	8	6	1	6	19	23	37
Bolton W	26	9	2	2	29	14	8	0	5	22	23	36
Aston Villa	26	10	0	3	63	23	5	0	8	26	33	30
Everton	26	8	2	3	33	22	4	2	7	17	27	28
Wolves	26	8	2	3	34	15	3	2	8	25	31	26
Burnley	26	9	1	3	34	14	2	3	8	15	31	26
Notts County	26	9	3	1	41	12	2	1	10	14	39	26
Blackburn R	26	8	3	2	39	26	2	3	8	19	39	26
Derby County	26	6	3	4	28	18	4	1	8	18	34	24
Accrington S	26	7	3	3	24	20	1	1	11	16	58	20
West Brom	26	6	3	4	37	24	0	3	10	14	34	18
Stoke City	26	5	0	8	19	19	0	4	9	19	42	14
Darwen	26	4	1	8	31	43	0	2	11	7	69	11

1892/93

	P	W	D	L	F	A	W	D	L	F	A	Pts
			Home						Away			
Sunderland	30	13	2	0	58	17	9	2	4	42	19	48
Preston NE	30	11	2	2	34	10	6	1	8	23	29	37
Everton	30	9	3	3	44	17	7	1	7	30	34	36
Aston Villa	30	12	1	2	50	24	4	2	9	23	38	35
Bolton W	30	12	1	2	43	21	1	5	9	13	34	32
Burnley	30	10	2	3	37	15	3	2	10	14	29	30
Stoke City	30	8	2	5	33	16	4	3	8	25	32	29
West Brom	30	9	2	4	35	17	3	3	9	23	52	29
Blackburn R	30	5	8	2	29	24	3	5	7	18	32	29
Nottingham F	30	7	2	6	30	27	3	6	6	18	25	28
Wolves	30	11	2	2	32	17	1	2	12	15	51	28
Sheffield W	30	8	2	5	34	28	4	1	10	21	37	27
Derby County	30	5	6	4	30	28	4	3	8	22	36	27
Notts County	30	8	3	4	34	15	2	1	12	19	46	24
Accrington	30	5	5	5	29	34	1	6	8	28	47	23
Man Utd	30	6	3	6	39	35	0	3	12	11	50	18

1894/95

	P		Home					Away				
	P	W	D	L	F	A	W	D	L	F	A	Pts
Sunderland	30	13	2	0	51	14	8	3	4	29	23	47
Everton	30	12	2	1	47	18	6	4	5	35	32	42
Aston Villa	30	12	2	1	51	12	5	3	7	31	31	39
Preston NE	30	9	3	3	32	14	6	2	7	30	32	35
Blackburn R	30	9	5	1	40	15	2	5	8	19	34	32
Sheffield Utd	30	10	2	3	33	17	4	2	9	24	38	32
Nottingham F	30	10	1	4	33	22	3	4	8	17	34	31
Sheffield Wed	30	10	2	3	36	19	2	2	11	14	36	28
Burnley	30	8	2	5	28	24	3	2	10	16	32	26
Bolton W	30	8	3	4	45	23	1	4	10	16	39	25
Wolves	30	7	4	4	24	25	2	3	10	19	38	25
Birmingham C	30	6	6	3	35	28	3	1	11	15	46	25
West Brom	30	9	2	4	38	21	1	2	12	13	45	24
Stoke City	30	7	3	5	35	25	2	3	10	15	42	24
Derby County	30	4	5	6	23	23	3	4	8	22	45	23
Liverpool	30	6	4	5	38	28	1	4	10	13	42	22

1901/02

	P		Home					Away				
	P	W	D	L	F	A	W	D	L	F	A	Pts
Sunderland	34	12	3	2	32	14	7	3	7	18	21	44
Everton	34	11	2	4	31	11	6	5	6	22	24	41
Newcastle Utd	34	11	3	3	41	14	3	6	8	7	20	37
Blackburn R	34	12	2	3	36	16	3	4	10	16	32	36
Nottingham F	34	11	4	2	32	13	2	5	10	11	30	35
Derby County	34	11	5	1	26	10	2	4	11	13	31	35
Bury	34	11	5	1	31	9	2	3	12	13	29	34
Aston Villa	34	9	5	3	27	13	4	3	10	15	27	34
Sheffield Wed	34	9	5	3	30	14	4	3	10	18	38	34
Sheffield Utd	34	10	5	2	38	13	3	2	12	15	35	33
Liverpool	34	8	3	6	28	16	2	9	6	14	22	32
Bolton W	34	10	6	1	38	17	2	2	13	13	39	32
Notts County	34	12	2	3	44	19	2	2	13	7	38	32
Wolves	34	12	3	2	32	13	1	3	13	14	44	32
Grimsby Town	34	11	3	3	33	16	2	3	12	11	44	32
Stoke City	34	10	4	3	31	12	1	5	11	14	43	31
Birmingham C	34	8	5	4	31	14	3	3	11	16	31	30
Manchester C	34	10	3	4	28	17	1	3	13	14	41	28

1912/13

	P	W	D	L	F	A	W	D	L	F	A	Pts
			Home						Away			
Sunderland	38	14	2	3	47	17	11	2	6	39	26	54
Aston Villa	38	13	4	2	57	21	6	8	5	29	31	50
Sheffield Wed	38	12	4	3	44	23	9	3	7	31	32	49
Man Utd	38	13	3	3	41	14	6	5	8	28	29	46
Blackburn R	38	10	5	4	54	21	6	8	5	25	22	45
Manchester C	38	12	3	4	34	15	6	5	8	19	22	44
Derby County	38	10	2	7	40	29	7	6	6	29	37	42
Bolton W	38	10	6	3	36	20	6	4	9	26	43	42
Oldham Ath	38	11	7	1	33	12	3	7	9	17	43	42
West Brom	38	8	7	4	30	20	5	5	9	27	30	38
Everton	38	8	2	9	28	31	7	5	7	20	23	37
Liverpool	38	12	2	5	40	24	4	3	12	21	47	37
Bradford City	38	10	5	4	33	22	2	6	11	17	38	35
Newcastle Utd	38	8	5	6	30	23	5	3	11	17	24	34
Sheffield Utd	38	10	5	4	36	24	4	1	14	20	46	34
Middlesboro'	38	6	9	4	29	22	5	1	13	26	47	32
Tottenham H	38	9	3	7	28	25	3	3	13	17	47	30
Chelsea	38	7	2	10	29	40	4	4	11	22	33	28
Notts County	38	6	4	9	19	20	1	5	13	9	36	23
Arsenal	38	1	8	10	11	31	2	4	13	15	43	18

1935/36

	P	W	D	L	F	A	W	D	L	F	A	Pts
			Home						Away			
Sunderland	42	17	2	2	71	33	8	4	9	38	41	56
Derby County	42	13	5	3	43	23	5	7	9	18	29	48
Huddersfield T	42	12	7	2	32	15	6	5	10	27	41	48
Stoke City	42	13	3	5	35	24	7	4	10	22	33	47
Brentford	42	11	5	5	48	25	6	7	8	33	35	46
Arsenal	42	9	9	3	44	22	6	6	9	34	26	45
Preston NE	42	15	3	3	44	18	3	5	13	23	46	44
Chelsea	42	11	7	3	39	27	4	6	11	26	45	43
Manchester C	42	13	2	6	44	17	4	6	11	24	43	42
Portsmouth	42	14	4	3	39	22	3	4	14	15	45	42
Leeds United	42	11	5	5	41	23	4	6	11	25	41	41
Birmingham C	42	10	6	5	38	31	5	5	11	23	32	41
Bolton W	42	11	4	6	41	27	3	9	9	26	49	41
Middlesboro'	42	12	6	3	56	23	3	4	14	28	47	40
Wolves	42	13	7	1	59	28	2	3	16	18	48	40

Everton	42	12	5	4	61	31	1	8	12	28	58	39
Grimsby Town	42	13	4	4	44	20	4	1	16	21	53	39
West Brom	42	12	3	6	54	31	4	3	14	35	57	38
Liverpool	42	11	4	6	43	23	2	8	11	17	41	38
Sheffield Wed	42	9	8	4	35	23	4	4	13	28	54	38
Aston Villa	42	7	6	8	47	56	6	3	12	34	54	35
Blackburn R	42	10	6	5	32	24	2	3	16	23	72	33

ELVIS HAS LEFT THE BUILDING

In the late 1970s, Sunderland's travelling support would, as is traditional in the North-East, do the rounds of the local pubs in anticipation of seeing the Black Cats in action.

On one particular occasion a group of supporters entertained themselves by not only ensuring that the local beer was fit for consumption but also playing music on the jukebox. One track in particular took their fancy and it was played over and over again. The singing spilled over into the stadium itself as the song was sung with gusto at first by the fans that had been in the pub and then picked up on by the whole travelling support. To this day the song 'Can't Help Falling in Love', made famous by Elvis Presley, can be heard not only by the supporters but also over the tannoy at the Stadium of Light to celebrate another Sunderland AFC victory.

As the song says 'wise men say only fools rush in but I can't help falling in love with you . . . Sunderland'.

As a postscript to this; Sunderland's rendition was picked up by supporters of other clubs and it spawned 'Blue Moon' at Manchester City, 'Delilah' at Stoke City and many more classic terrace anthems.

A CANARY SAVES THE DAY

In the early days of Sunderland AFC the club was so strapped for cash that it was seriously mooted that they would go out of business.

As luck would have it, it was alleged that one of the directors had a prize canary that he offered up for raffle. Ironically the canary was won by the director who owned it and he raffled it again.

The result was that enough money was raised to save the club from financial oblivion. Quite literally, a canary saved the day!

SUNDERLAND IN THE LEAGUE CUP

In October 1960 Sunderland played their first game in the League Cup competition. They lost 4–3 at Brentford. The following is our entire record in the competition.

	Pld	W	D	L	Other	F	A
Arsenal	3	1	0	2	0	3	6
Aston Villa	4	0	1	3	0	3	9
Blackburn	2	1	0	1	0	4	4
Blackpool	1	1	0	0	0	4	1
Bolton	2	1	1	0	0	2	1
Bournemouth	2	1	1	0	0	2	1
Bradford City	1	0	0	1	0	1	2
Brentford	1	0	0	1	0	3	4
Bristol City	2	1	0	1	0	6	2
Bristol Rovers	2	1	0	1	0	3	4
Bury	3	2	0	1	0	4	4
Bye	1	0	0	0	1	0	0
Cambridge	3	3	0	0	0	14	5
Chelsea	2	2	0	0	0	5	2
Cheltenham Town	1	1	0	0	0	1	0
Chester City	5	4	1	0	0	10	1
Coventry	3	0	1	2	0	2	9
Crewe Alexandra	1	0	1	0	0	3	3
Crystal Palace	4	1	1	2	0	3	4
Derby County	4	1	2	1	0	6	9
Everton	2	1	1	0	0	4	3
Exeter City	2	1	1	0	0	7	4
Fulham	2	1	1	0	0	4	1
Grimsby Town	1	1	0	0	0	2	1
Halifax	1	1	0	0	0	3	2
Huddersfield	5	1	0	4	0	6	13

	Pld	W	D	L	Other	F	A
Hull City	1	1	0	0	0	2	1
Leeds United	3	2	0	1	0	4	4
Leicester City	2	0	1	1	0	2	3
Lincoln City	1	0	0	1	0	1	2
Liverpool	3	0	0	3	0	0	5
Luton Town	5	4	0	1	0	11	5
Manchester City	2	1	1	0	0	2	1
Manchester United	4	1	2	1	0	6	6
Mansfield Town	1	1	0	0	0	2	1
Middlesbrough	5	1	1	3	0	3	7
Millwall	2	0	1	1	0	2	3
Newcastle United	2	0	2	0	0	4	4
Northampton Town	1	0	1	0	0	2	2
Norwich	6	0	2	4	0	3	10
Nottingham Forest	3	2	1	0	0	4	2
Notts County	1	0	0	1	0	1	2
Oldham	1	1	0	0	0	7	1
Portsmouth	2	1	1	0	0	2	1
Preston	3	1	1	1	0	4	5
Rotherham	2	1	1	0	0	5	3
Scunthorpe	1	1	0	0	0	2	0
Sheffield United	4	1	1	2	0	3	5
Sheffield Wednesday	1	0	0	1	0	2	4
Stockport	2	0	1	1	0	2	3
Stoke City	2	0	0	2	0	0	5
Swansea	1	0	0	1	0	1	3
Swindon	2	1	0	1	0	4	5
Tottenham	3	1	1	1	0	3	3
Walsall	3	3	0	0	0	13	4
Watford	3	3	0	0	0	4	0
West Ham United	5	1	1	3	0	7	9
Wimbledon	1	0	0	1	0	2	3
Wolverhampton	2	1	1	0	0	6	1
York City	6	4	1	1	0	13	6
Totals	146	60	33	52	1	234	214

THE GREATEST CENTRE-HALF?

Charlie Hurley

'King' Charlie was voted player of the century by Sunderland football fans on 25 November 1979 at the Mayfair Ballroom, to coincide with the centenary celebrations. He was born in Cork, Republic of Ireland, in October 1936 and is still a popular figure on Wearside today, although he now lives in the south of England.

The King was only seven months old when he moved from his native country to Rainham in Essex to eventually be signed by Millwall, the Lions from The Den.

On 26 September 1957, Charlie Hurley strode into Roker Park to begin a career that would span twelve seasons and 402 appearances. It is a little-known fact that when originally asked by Millwall whether he would like a move, he initially turned Sunderland down. The £18,000 transfer was sealed due to the apparent persuasiveness of then Sunderland manager Alan Brown, who had been alerted to his potential by the former Millwall manager Charlie Hewitt.

The King's Sunderland career met with a disastrous start; a 7–0 rout by Blackpool, coupled with him scoring an own goal on his debut. This was quickly followed by a 6–0 thrashing from Burnley. By the end of the third game, a 0–0 draw against Preston North End, a young Charlie must have wondered what had hit him.

Charlie had been unfortunate enough to have competed against centre-forwards who would later go on to represent England. In Ray Charnley and Ray Pointer, Blackpool and Burnley had strikers of the highest quality. It was a baptism of fire.

Things of course would get better, and eventually promotion would be achieved in the 1963/64 season after two heartbreaking campaigns which had seen Sunderland miss out on top flight football due to consecutive last-day failures against Swansea Town and Chelsea.

Away from Sunderland, Charlie made his debut for Eire (as was) at the tender age of twenty, having previously been unable to make an international call up due to injury one year earlier.

Overall he would gain 40 caps for his native country, 33 while on Wearside, and would have the honour of captaining them.

Curiously, for a man who was indelibly linked with powerful headed goals, it took 124 league and cup appearances for Sunderland before he 'broke his scoring duck'. A 1–1 Boxing Day draw in 1960 against Sheffield United was the catalyst for 42 more goals.

The crowd would of course hold its breath when the Lads were awarded a corner, and the chants of 'Charlie, Charlie' echoed around Roker Park as he began his journey from his centre-half position to the opponents' penalty box. Quite what opposition centre-forwards and full-backs made of him is a moot point.

While the 1963/64 season was special for Sunderland AFC, resulting in promotion, it was also personally highly satisfactory for the King. Only the late, great Bobby Moore prevented Hurley from becoming Football Writers Player of the Year; the runners up placing truly testifying that, at his peak, there was no finer centre-half in English football.

An article on Charlie would not be complete without mentioning the famous Sunderland half-back line that complemented each other so well. In Martin Harvey, Charlie Hurley and of course Jimmy McNab, it's doubtful whether a Sunderland trio since has been so defensively effective.

In the first game following the 1963/64 promotion season, a now managerless Sunderland started the campaign with a 3–3 draw at Leicester City. Derek Forster became the youngest player in Football League history to play, when an injury to Jimmy Montgomery thrust the young keeper into the fray at the tender age of fifteen years and 185 days old. Hurley's experience that day must have been invaluable.

Alan Brown's departure from Roker Park, to take over at Sheffield Wednesday, saw first George Hardwick and then Scotsman Ian McColl replace him. During one match at Old Trafford in November 1966, first Hurley and then northern Ireland defender John Parke went in goal, as Monty retired from the game through an injury sustained in the first half.

Hurley's last goal for Sunderland came against Arsenal in April 1968, typically a header. His last appearance in a red and white shirt was at Turf Moor, Burnley, in April 1969.

Hurley's greatest match was probably the FA Cup fifth-round victory at Carrow Road in February 1961, when he scored the only goal to dump Norwich City out of the competition. Famously, Sunderland would then go on to succumb to a Danny Blanchflower inspired spurs side, who became double winners for the first time in the twentieth century.

On 2 June 1969, Charlie was transferred to Bolton Wanderers on a free transfer.

SUNDERLAND IN THE FA CUP

Sunderland's very first game in the FA Cup was in November 1884, against Redcar. They lost 3–1. The following is Sunderland AFC's entire record in the FA Cup. It includes the abandoned game against Manchester City in 1912/13 and also the scratched game against Sunderland Albion.

	Total	W	D	L	Other	F	A
Accrington Stanley	2	2	0	0	0	6	1
Arsenal	5	2	1	2	0	6	7
Aston Villa	9	1	1	7	0	11	23
Birmingham City	9	2	2	5	0	8	14
Blackburn Rovers	12	0	6	6	0	11	22
Blackpool	1	1	0	0	0	1	0
Bolton Wanderers	8	5	2	1	0	14	6
Boston United	1	1	0	0	0	8	1
Bradford City	1	1	0	0	0	1	0
Bradford Park Avenue	2	2	0	0	0	4	1
Brentford	2	1	0	1	0	6	4
Bristol City	2	2	0	0	0	10	3
Bristol Rovers	1	0	0	1	0	0	1
Burnley	12	5	4	3	0	13	12
Bury	3	2	0	1	0	10	6
Cardiff City	5	1	2	2	0	5	7
Carlisle United	6	2	3	1	0	6	4
Chatham	1	1	0	0	0	9	0
Chelsea	2	1	1	0	0	3	2
Chesterfield	2	1	0	1	0	3	2
Clapton Orient	1	1	0	0	0	6	0

	Total	W	D	L	Other	F	A
Coventry City	3	2	0	1	0	5	3
Crewe Alexandra	1	1	0	0	0	2	0
Crystal Palace	6	3	2	1	0	7	4
Darlington	1	1	0	0	0	2	0
Darwen	1	1	0	0	0	2	0
Derby County	4	1	2	1	0	9	7
Doncaster Rovers	1	0	0	1	0	0	2
Elswick Rangers	1	1	0	0	0	5	3
Everton	14	4	3	7	0	16	28
Exeter City	2	1	1	0	0	5	3
Fairfield	1	1	0	0	0	11	1
Fulham	2	1	0	1	0	4	6
Gainsborough Trinity	2	1	1	0	0	4	1
Gravesend	2	1	1	0	0	6	3
Grimsby Town	2	2	0	0	0	5	2
Hartlepool United	1	1	0	0	0	1	0
Huddersfield Town	2	1	0	1	0	7	3
Hull City	3	3	0	0	0	9	2
Ipswich Town	2	2	0	0	0	3	1
Leeds United	6	2	2	2	0	7	7
Leicester City	1	0	0	1	0	0	1
Leicester Fosse	1	1	0	0	0	4	1
Leyton Orient	1	0	0	1	0	0	3
Lincoln City	1	1	0	0	0	1	0
Liverpool	5	1	1	3	0	3	11
Luton Town	6	4	2	0	0	11	3
Manchester City	9	2	2	4	1	13	11
Manchester United	9	0	5	4	0	13	22
Middlesbrough	6	3	2	1	0	12	9
Millwall	2	1	0	1	0	2	2
Morpeth Harriers	2	2	0	0	0	7	4
New Brompton	1	0	0	1	0	1	3
Newcastle East End	1	1	0	0	0	2	0
Newcastle United	7	2	3	2	0	9	8
Newcastle West End	3	2	0	1	0	5	3
Newport County	1	1	0	0	0	2	0
Northampton Town	3	2	1	0	0	8	3
Northwich Victoria	1	1	0	0	0	3	0
Norwich City	7	4	1	2	0	11	8

	Total	W	D	L	Other	F	A
Nottingham Forest	6	1	1	4	0	9	14
Notts County	7	4	2	1	0	13	6
Oldham Athletic	2	1	0	1	0	3	2
Oxford United	3	1	1	1	0	4	5
Peterborough United	1	1	0	0	0	7	1
Plymouth Argyle	3	3	0	0	0	8	2
Portsmouth	1	1	0	0	0	1	0
Port Vale	5	1	2	2	0	6	7
Preston North End	9	7	1	1	0	22	8
Queens Park Rangers	1	1	0	0	0	4	0
Reading	3	1	1	1	0	5	4
Redcar	2	0	0	2	0	1	6
Rotherham United	3	2	1	0	0	7	2
Royal Arsenal	1	1	0	0	0	6	0
Scunthorpe United	3	1	1	1	0	4	4
Sheffield United	8	6	1	1	0	13	7
Sheffield Wednesday	7	2	1	4	0	5	5
Southampton	9	5	2	2	0	16	11
Stoke City	9	2	5	2	0	12	10
Sunderland Albion	1	0	0	0	1	0	0
Swansea	3	2	1	0	0	6	2
Swindon Town	1	1	0	0	0	4	2
Tottenham Hotspur	7	1	1	5	0	6	19
Tranmere Rovers	2	0	0	2	0	0	2
Watford	2	1	0	1	0	1	1
West Bromwich Albion	4	0	0	4	0	5	10
West Ham United	4	1	1	2	0	4	5
Wigan Athletic	1	0	0	1	0	0	3
Wimbledon	2	0	0	2	0	2	4
Wolves	8	2	4	2	0	12	9
Woolwich Arsenal	1	0	0	1	0	0	5
Wrexham	2	0	1	1	0	2	3
Yeovil Town	1	0	0	1	0	1	2
York City	2	1	1	0	0	2	1
Totals	335	142	79	112	2	549	446

LUCKIEST LEAGUE GROUNDS

Although Sunderland fans might struggle to believe this, we do have some lucky grounds! Based on a minimum qualification of ten league matches played, here are the top ten luckiest grounds for Sunderland AFC in order of win ratio – i.e. number of wins to matches played:

Grimsby Town
Pld 24   W 12   D 6   L 6   F 37   A 33
Maybe it's the sea air that reminds Sunderland and their fans of home, or maybe some properties of the local haddock, but a trip to Grimsby is a one to look forward to. The clubs first visit for league points was in 1901 – a 3–3 draw – and from 1938 to 1988 Sunderland never lost in ten visits. This, however, was due retribution to the inexplicable 6–0 defeat just a few days before the 1937 FA Cup Final.

Luton Town
Pld 23   W 11   D 2   L 10   F 42   A 49
It is quite remarkable that this ground is high up on the list of lucky venues for the club as the first three visits ended in 8–2, 6–2 and 7–1 hammerings. However, in the next ten visits Sunderland lost only twice. Revenge was sweet in 2007 when Sunderland, under the stewardship of Roy Keane, walloped the Hatters 5–0 to claim the football League Championship and promotion at the very first attempt.

Bradford City
Pld 19   W 9   D 2   L 8   F 34   A 23
Sunderland's first visit to City was in 1908 and resulted in a 2–0 win. Then, from 1909 to 1989, Sunderland won just twice in twelve visits. Since 1990 however, the Black Cats have won six on the trot at Valley Parade, scoring eighteen goals in the process and conceding just one. Bradford have watched helplessly on four of those occasions where they have conceded four to the rampant red and whites.

Barnsley

Pld 12   W 5   D 1   L 6   F 12   A 15

Sunderland didn't visit Barnsley for league points until 1959 and won on that visit. They didn't return until 1985 and until 1995, in what was a poor spell for Sunderland history-wise, they won just once. However, the last three trips have all been won to stand at a win ratio of 42 per cent.

Fulham

Pld 23   W 9   D 5   L 9   F 31   A 33

Sunderland's first trip to Craven Cottage was in a thirteen match unbeaten run that saw them top the then First Division. Running out 3–0 winners, they remained unbeaten in their next two visits. A run of five consecutive defeats, one a 6–2 hammering, was stopped with a no-score draw in 1972 and the next ten visits resulted in just one defeat.

Oxford United

Pld 13   W 5   D 4   L 4   F 13   A 15

With a win ratio of 38 per cent, Sunderland's trips to Oxford started poorly when they won only once in the first five visits. However, the last eight visits have proved fruitful with just one defeat in that time.

Bury

Pld 28   W 10   D 5   L 13   F 39   A 48

Undefeated in 54 per cent of their league trips to Gigg Lane, Sunderland first visited Bury as far back as 1896. An initial 2–1 victory set us up for just two defeats in our first six games there. Unbeaten there since 1962, our last four visits have produced 10 goals which included a Kevin Phillips inspired 5–2 rout in 1999.

Hull City

Pld 14   W 5   D 3   L 6   F 18   A 21

Sunderland didn't make their first journey to Hull until 1960. Although there are six defeats in the fourteen games, when Sunderland win at Hull they usually win well. An example of that was the 2008/09 4–1 defeat of the home side, and the 1976 trip that resulted in the same scoreline.

Leicester City

Pld 39   W 12   D 6   L 21   F 47   A 71

Sunderland supporters will no doubt be surprised too see Leicester City feature on any list of lucky grounds as far as the Black Cats are concerned, but the red and whites have returned from the City of Leicester with something in almost 50 per cent of their trips. Sunderland first visited Leicester in 1909 when City was then known as Fosse. The first skirmish with them as City was in 1925.

Middlesbrough

Pld 64   W 19   D 17   L 28   F 80   A 101

Sunderland first played Middlesbrough at the old Ayresome Park ground in 1902, and in the first forty-four visits to the stadium for a Tees–Wear game, lost 'only' sixteen times, winning seventeen, other results including a 5–5 draw in 1936. However, from 1972 to 2002 Sunderland won only once, although since 1994 Sunderland has lost only three times in the last ten league visits to their near neighbours.

NO KNOWLEDGE OF FOOTBALL?

In 1955 Sunderland legend Len Shackleton wrote his autobiography. Chapter nine, entitled 'The Average Director's Knowledge of Football', was a blank page, deliberately left blank in accordance with the author's wishes!

BAD TEETH

Following the 1937 FA Cup Final at Wembley, where Sunderland defeated Preston North End 3–1, a member of the Board of the Royal Free Hospital in London, Sir Thomas McAra, commented that from his observations two out of every three Sunderland supporters at the match either had no front teeth or badly decayed front teeth.

While it was a curious remark to make, it emphasised the lack of dedicated dental care in the North-East.

THE MAN WHO COUNTS

At the heart of every football club is the chairman, the man who takes the blame and takes the plaudits when it all goes right or it all goes wrong. Here is a list of Sunderland AFC chairmen and their records of success or otherwise since the club entered the professional league in 1890:

	Seasons		1	2	3	R	FA	LC
Thompson	1890/91	1894/95	5					3
Henderson	1895/96	1902/03	8					1
Todd	1903/04		1					
Taylor	1904/05	1912/13	9					1
Wilson	1913/14	1920/21	4					
Bell	1921/22	1929/30	9					
Raine	1930/31	1937/38	8				1	1
White	1938/39	1939/40	1					
Prior	1940/41	1948/49	3					
Ditchburn	1949/50	1956/57	8					
Turnbull	1957/58		1			1		
Ritson	1958/59	1959/60		2				
Collings S	1960/61	1967/68	4	4				
Parker	1968/69	1970/71	2	1		1		
Collings K	1971/72	1979/80	1	8		1	1	1
Cowie	1980/81	1985/86	5	1		1		
Murray	1986/87	1992/93	2	4	1	2		1
Featherstone	1993/94	1994/95		2				
Murray	1995/96	2005/06	6	5		3		3
Quinn	2006/07	2008/09	2	1				1
Totals			79	28	1	9	2	12

Key:
1, 2 or 3	Tier
R	Relegated
FA	FA Cup Winners
LC	League Champions

SACKED!

When Sunderland played Aston Villa in February 1921 at Roker Park it was an eagerly awaited game for a number of reasons, not least that ace marksman Charlie Buchan was in fine goalscoring form for the Black Cats. As a result, many workers left the shipyards that day to go over to Roker Park. Unfortunately some were found out and promptly sacked by their employers!

THE WRONG SCORE

While the media today has access to instant television coverage and action replays and the internet gives up-to-date information on football results, it obviously wasn't always that way.

When Sunderland played Jesmond on 10 January 1885 it was reported three days after the game that Sunderland won 1–0. However, the following week that was retracted and the correct result given as a victory for Jesmond.

Quite often match reports of the day carried different goalscorers in different newspapers for the same match.

ENGLAND ON WEARSIDE

England have played a number of times on Wearside in full internationals. The first game they played was at the Newcastle Road ground in 1891 when they defeated Wales 4–1. Their next visit, in 1899, resulted in their highest ever recorded victory; 13–2 against Northern Ireland.

England's latest full international, and probably the last for a long time (due to the completion of the new Wembley Stadium), was against Turkey at the Stadium of Light in 2003 for a European Championship qualification game. England won 2–0.

PENALTY!

In England, the first ever penalty shoot-out in a professional match took place in 1970 at Boothferry Park, Hull, between Hull City and Manchester United during the semi-final of the Watney Cup, and was won by Manchester United. The first player to take a kick was George Best, and the first to miss was Denis Law.

Sunderland's very first penalty shoot-out occurred in 1979. The following is the full listing of penalty shootouts that Sunderland have been involved in:

5/9/1979	v. Newcastle Utd	League Cup	W 7–6
1/10/1985	v. Grimsby Town	Full Members' Cup	W 3–2
4/11/1985	v. Manchester C	Full Members' Cup	L 4–3
16/9/1986	v. Barnsley	Full Members' Cup	W 8–7
11/12/1990	v. Notts County	ZDS Cup	W 3–1
25/5/1998	v. Charlton Ath	Play-off final	L 7–6
11/11/1998	v. Everton	League Cup	W 5–4
5/2/2003	v. Blackburn R	FA Cup	W 3–0
17/5/2004	v. Crystal Palace	Play-off semi-final	L 5–4
21/9/2004	v. Crewe A	League Cup	L 4–2
23/9/2008	v. Northampton T	League Cup	W 4–3

SPONSORS

For a club such as Sunderland there has always been a variety of firms prepared to enter into sponsorship deals with the football club. Those chosen firms have stayed loyal to the football club as the following short list testifies to, just four shirt sponsors in twenty-six years:

1983 to 1985	Cowies
1985 to 1999	Vaux Breweries
1999 to 2007	Reg Vardy
2007 to 2009	Boylesports

SUNDERLAND STALWARTS

While the modern day footballer may not have much of a reputation for hanging around long at any one football club, it didn't used to be that way. Sunderland has had some loyal servants over the years such as:

Jimmy Montgomery	627 appearances
Len Ashurst	458
Ted Doig	457
Stan Anderson	447
Gary Bennett	443
Bobby Kerr	433
Gordon Armstrong	416
Charlie Buchan	411
Michael Gray	410
Charlie Hurley	401

YOUNG GUNS

Up until recently, Sunderland had a decent record of giving young up and coming football talent a chance. Here are the youngest players ever to play a first team game for Sunderland along with their age at the time:

	Age		Debut
Derek Forster	15 years	185 days	1964
James Hamilton	16	103	1971
Cecil Irwin	16	166	1958
Rob Hindmarch	16	262	1978
Nick Sharkey	16	341	1960
James Davison	17	20	1959
James Thorpe	17	39	1930
Barry Venison	17	55	1981
Joe Bolton	17	75	1972
Fred Bett	17	97	1938

GOALKEEPER DIES

Following the end of the Chelsea match on 1 February 1936, the Sunderland goalkeeper Jimmy Thorpe collapsed at home and spent all of the following Monday in bed, very seriously ill as a result of a kick he sustained in the match. He had a head wound, swollen eye and a badly bruised face. He was later admitted to the Monkwearmouth and Southwick Hospital and died on Wednesday 5 February.

The previous professional player in England to die as a result of a footballing injury was S. Raleigh of Gillingham who passed away in December 1934 as a result of concussion. In September 1931, the Glasgow Celtic goalkeeper, Thomson, had died following a fractured skull sustained in the Old Firm game against Glasgow Rangers.

On Monday 10 February Thorpe was buried at Jarrow Cemetery, the cortège leaving 11 York Avenue, Monkton, the home of his in-laws, at 2.30 p.m. The funeral was attended by all of the Sunderland players and directors with the former acting as under bearers.

Local residents, his community, lined the streets four deep along the way to the cemetery to honour the young goalkeeper. As well as expected wreaths from Sunderland AFC there were others from Chelsea, Everton, Newcastle United and Sunderland Police Recreation Club.

An inquest into Thorpe's passing which commenced on 13 February under the direction of the coroner J.C. Morton, gave the cause of death as due to Diabetes 'accelerated by the rough usage he received in the game and that the referee was very lax in his control of the game.'

Jimmy's Father had confirmed that his son had sugar diabetes and had previously spent a four week spell in hospital as a result of his condition. The inquest focussed on a particular incident in the game that was graphically described where one moment Thorpe was kneeling in the goalmouth but, following a rush by four Chelsea players, the young goalkeeper was left sprawled out and lay there for 'a second or two' as the opposition players had kicked him repeatedly to try and get the ball. Sunderland players such as Murray had immediately come to Thorpe's aid and legitimately shoulder-charged the Chelsea players as they tried to protect their team mate.

As a result of what the coroner heard he urged the Board of the Football Association to instruct all referees that they must exercise stricter control over the players so as to eliminate as far as possible any future accidents.

On 17 February 1936 the Football Association set up a commission to look into Thorpe's untimely death. For the commission both Sunderland and Chelsea were required to submit their observations on the game. However, the commission was in effect a whitewash with the referee being exonerated and, rather incredibly, Sunderland were blamed for allowing Thorpe to play, despite evidence from the club's doctor that Thorpe was known to be in good health, despite his diabetes.

Sunderland were subsequently crowned league champions and on 7 May 1936 the club held a celebratory dinner at which Thorpe's widow and mother were in attendance. Jimmy's championship medal was duly presented to them.

Thorpe had joined Sunderland from his home-town team Jarrow aged seventeen on 26 September 1930. He was talented enough to be selected for the first eleven after just two games for the reserves and was rumoured to be a likely England selection at the time of his death. He made a total of 139 league and cup appearances for Sunderland.

He died aged just twenty-two, leaving a wife, May, and a three-year-old son, Ronnie.

As a postscript to Jimmy's death, it was all too much for his mother Emily. Bereft at her son's death she passed away herself soon after.

THE 1913 FA CUP FINAL: THE BACKGROUND STORIES

In 1913 Sunderland reached the FA Cup Final where they were defeated 1–0 by Aston Villa at Crystal Palace. As you would imagine there were one or two stories that would subsequently emerge in the years after the match that are worth noting:

Walter Tinsley

Sunderland player George Holley had been carrying an ankle injury and was not expected to play in the Cup Final. Indeed, there is a very famous picture of the Sunderland players in civilian clothes, lining up at leisure the day before, that shows Holley wearing football boots rather than normal shoes. Charlie Buchan later explained that he was testing his ankle out constantly to see if he could be fit enough to play but in the end looked to have succumbed to defeat.

However, in the hour before the game, Walter Tinsley, Holley's replacement, was rumoured to be so overcome with nerves having seen the massive crowd, that he couldn't play, so Holley was an eleventh hour team-member, passed fit to play.

Tommy Barber

Barber was a Geordie who was born in West Stanley towards the outskirts of the Newcastle city limits. For him it was a poignant moment to score the winner against Newcastle's arch-rivals Sunderland AFC.

Sam Hardy, the Aston Villa goalkeeper, had dreamt before the final that Barber would score the winning goal and so it transpired. For Barber though, near tragedy would strike during his service in the First World War.

At the Somme, Barber was carried from the battlefield, presumed dead, and so a myth perpetuated that he had indeed passed away. In fact, although poisoned by mustard gas, Barber made a recovery turning out for non-league teams such as Stalybridge Celtic and Crystal Palace when hostilities ended. Barber did return to league football briefly with both Merthyr Town and Walsall but it didn't last long, the gas had taken its toll on Tommy's body. He died in 1925, aged just thirty-nine.

The Charity Shield

The Charity Shield was first played for in 1908 and was an evolution from the original Sheriff of London Shield played between the League Champions and the amateur equivalent (Southern League Champions). Due to the furore surrounding the events of the FA Cup Final, where the Sunderland captain Charlie Thomson fought a running battle with Villa's Hampton, the FA did not invite Sunderland to play Plymouth Argyle in 1914.

Penalty Miss

The FA Cup Final penalty miss by Wallace was ultimately inconsequential. However, it was a rare feat and would not be repeated for another seventy-five years.

Disgraceful Authorities

Following the match the Football Association's handling of the fixture was lambasted by the media and public alike. Over 2,000 spectators were turned away from what was not an all-ticket match, with many injured trying to gain admittance. One newspaper was quoted as saying, 'The arrangements were of a primitive type and a disgrace to the authorities. Imperfect terracing was in a shocking state, the foot holding being treacherously insecure.'

Sunderland's Reception

After the match the Sunderland players, officials and invited guests attended a banquet at the Trocadero Restaurant on Shaftesbury Avenue, London, near to the West End Theatres. Sunderland director W.H. Bell proposed a toast to 'the Football Association and kindred bodies.' In response an FA official suggested that there were four things special about Sunderland AFC: The directors, who were the best men in the Borough of Sunderland; No club had a better relationship between the players and directors; There was a great bond between the town and the football club, and no one had a better chairman (Fred Taylor) than Sunderland. There was much applause.

Sunderland AFC's Overdraft

At the reception Fred Taylor confirmed that at the beginning of the 1912/13 campaign Sunderland had a confirmed bank overdraft of £12,000. As a result of the revenues gained during the FA Cup run, Sunderland ended the season debt-free.

Record Crowd

Confusion surrounded the official crowd at Sydenham. On the day the crowd was given as 121,919 although this was later revised to 120,081. Whatever, it was still a world record crowd for a football match, eclipsing the 110,802 that had watched the 1901 Spurs v. Sheffield United 2–2 draw.

IT'S JUST NOT CRICKET

As well as being an outstanding footballer for Sunderland from 1946 to 1954, Willie Watson also played cricket for England.

HOME SWEET HOME

Once upon a time, Wearside was considered a relative fortress for Sunderland AFC. The following are some miscellaneous records from our home league games since 1890:

Most home wins in a season	19	1998/99 and 1975/76
Fewest home wins in a season	1	2005/06
Most home draws in a season	12	1994/95
Fewest home draws in a season	0	1891/92 and 1908/09
Most home defeats in a season	14	2002/03 and 2005/06
Fewest home defeats in a season	0	1891/92, 1892/93, 1894/95, 1895/96, 1975/76, 1979/80
Most home goals in a season	71	1935/36
Fewest home goals in a season	11	2002/03

RED AND WHITE STRIPES

The one thing that makes most teams instantly recognisable is their traditional strip. However, the evolution to the famous red and white stripes that are worn by the Sunderland team is consistent with many clubs in that it wasn't the first outfit that they wore. Here we chart the evolution of the Sunderland strip and the change to red and white stripes.

The original colours worn by Sunderland from 1879 to 1884 was an all blue strip, undoubtedly in due deference to Sunderland's first home ground at the Blue House Field, Hendon (could you really wear any other colour playing at a ground with such a name?).

The team wore a blue top, blue shorts and either blue socks or, in the case of those who didn't fancy having their legs broken in those days (rough tackling was the norm), shin pads that have the distinct look of something akin to cricket pads about them. They certainly weren't the lightweight, hardly-seen modern versions.

On Saturday 13 December 1884, a good crowd, about 500, including a sprinkling of ladies, saw Sunderland turn out against Castle Eden in new colours of red and white halved tops. The local newspaper, the *Sunderland Echo*, decided that this was a great improvement on the blue strip but they wondered why Sunderland had chosen those colours which another unnamed club in the county already wore. The new outfit brought Sunderland good luck as they defeated Castle Eden 8–1.

Why Sunderland all of a sudden moved to red and white is a moot point and for which there is no immediate answer. A variety of shorts were worn, some dark and some light.

By 1886/87 the strip had evolved, not much, but this time the red part of the red and white halved top was now on the left-hand side.

It had always been thought that as Sunderland wore the soon to be famous red and white stripes during the 1887/88 season, they naturally wore them on the opening day of the season against Notts Mellors. However, subsequent research has proved this to be incorrect. The strip was actually worn for the first time in the third game of the season, against Darlington St Augustine's on Saturday 24 September 1887. The team had their picture taken in their splendid new outfit before the game. It brought good luck and a 1–0 victory. The *Newcastle Daily Chronicle* reported that, 'Darlington St Augustine's visited Sunderland for the first time this season on a fine day for a game which drew a crowd of fully 4,000 spectators to Newcastle Road. The home side wore their new uniform of red and white vertical stripes and white knickers for the first time and they looked very pretty when they took the field. The sides were well represented but O'Hare of Darlington failed to appear and Erskine of Sunderland guested for the visitors. The visitors won the toss and elected to play down the slope.'

The game, however, wasn't so lucky for one unfortunate fan. Towards the close of the game a sad incident took place which cast gloom over proceedings. It seemed a forty-year-old man named James Cowan of Cornhill in Southwick fell to the ground as if in a fit. He was rushed to the pavilion and was immediately attended to by Dr Pearcy who was at the ground, but regrettably his services were of no avail as the man was dead having apparently suffered an epileptic fit. The deceased was a foreman at Messrs Laing & Co. Shipbuilding Yard.

WHERE ARE THEY NOW?

Following the 1978 World Cup it became fashionable for English clubs to sign Argentinian players. Sunderland AFC joined in when they paid a reported then club record £320,000 to Atlético Huracán for their midfield maestro Claudio Marangoni during the 1979/80 season. He notched his first goal for the club against Shrewsbury in December 1979.

Plainly ill-at-ease in the old Second Division, he left Sunderland twelve months later and the years since his departure saw him cast as a 'failure' in English football. However, on looking at his subsequent career we find that he went on to win nine full caps for Argentina.

Marangoni played one season for Huracán before joining Club Atlético Independiente in 1982. He won three major titles with the club, the 1983 Metropolitano followed by the Copa Libertadores and Copa Intercontinental in 1984 (World Club Championship). In 1988 he left Independiente to join Boca Juniors where he won a further two international tournaments, the Supercopa Sudamericana 1989 and the Recopa Sudamericana 1990.

He was voted in the top thirty most influential players for Boca Juniors during the period from the 1970s to the 1990s, alongside legends such as Diego Maradona.

When his playing days ended, Marangoni then went on to form the Escuela Modelo de Futbol y Deportes in Buenos Aires with a business partner, Julio Bocca. It is a school, soccer and sports club for children that also specialises in swimming, rhythmic gymnastics, tennis, fitness and dance that is sponsored by firms such as Pepsi and Adidas.

Marangoni has also been invited as a key speaker at conferences, most notably in October 2008, where he gave his views on 'Investing in football clubs and club takeovers'. Not bad for a 'failure'.

25 APRIL: A BUSY DAY

25/4/98 Kevin Phillips scores twice in a 3–0 win over Stoke in the last home game of the season.

25/4/93 Newcastle United 1–0 Sunderland. Less said about this one the better.

25/4/92 Anton Rogan scores his only goal for the club in a 2–2 draw at the Goldstone Ground. Don Goodman gets the other.

25/4/87 Gary Bennett scores the only goal in a 1–0 win at Shrewsbury.

25/4/81 Alan Brown scores against Brighton, but Sunderland concede a goal with almost the last kick of the match to lose 2–1. Needing a win at Anfield to stay up, Sunderland would pull off the impossible!

25/4/79 Sunderland 6–2 Sheffield United. Wilf Rostron scores a hat-trick and Barry Siddall saves a last minute penalty to preserve the four-goal win Sunderland need to top the table on goal difference. There was to be last day heartbreak though.

25/4/72 Ian Porterfield and Bobby Kerr score as Sunderland come back from a half-time deficit to beat Carlisle 2–1 at Brunton Park

25/4/66 Neil Martin scores in a 2–1 defeat at relegated Northampton Town.

25/4/64 Brian Usher and Nick Sharkey score as Sunderland finish their first ever promotion season with a 2–2 draw at Grimsby.

25/4/36 Sunderland are beaten 4–0 at Derby County but it doesn't matter. SAFC are Football League Champions!

THEY SAID IT ...

'Nonetheless, we were faced with a situation where our fans were stranded and needed assistance. The club was happy to provide transport back to the North-East for the group, which included children, elderly and disabled fans as their safety and well-being was paramount. Thankfully everyone returned home safely and we'll now draw a line under this and any fans who may still feel aggrieved with the situation – remember, the three points came home as well.

The revered Sunderland chairman Niall Quinn gives his verdict on the episode which resulted in the football club paying for stranded SAFC fans to come back home from Bristol Airport in taxis, having watched the Black Cats win at Cardiff City. The bill? A reported £8,000!

DID YOU KNOW?

Club founder James Allan holds the record for scoring the most goals in a single match for Sunderland AFC, a staggering twelve.

During the latter part of the nineteenth century, Sunderland AFC won the Durham Association Challenge Cup four times in five seasons.

Sunderland AFC were the inaugural winners of the Football League First Division in 1892/93.

When Sunderland AFC defeated Newcastle United 9–1 at St James' Park in 1908, they scored 6 goals in just 10 minutes!

Ernie England played 351 games for Sunderland AFC and never scored a solitary goal. This is a club record for an outfield player.

ONE HUNDRED AND COUNTING

During Sunderland AFC's 100th league season, 2000/01:

Sunderland:
Played their 2,000th home league game (v. Middlesbrough).
Played their 2,000th away league game (v. Leeds United).
Played their 4,000th league game (at Elland Road).
Saw their top striker break the clubs post-war goalscoring record – Kevin Phillips.
Recorded the second highest average home crowd in the club's history.
Scored their 2,500th away league goal (Kevin Phillips v. Chelsea).
Recorded their 150th Premiership point (v Southampton).
Scored their 100th Premiership goal.
Witnessed their first player to play in 100 Premiership matches – Michael Gray.
Saw the 450th competitive goal scored by a Peter Reid SAFC team (third goal v. Charlton).
Delighted at the 150th SAFC league goal scored at Stadium of Light (Niall Quinn v. Charlton).
Were disappointed at Stadium of Light's 250th competitive goal (Jensen for Charlton).
Were disappointed at the 200th league goal scored at Stadium of Light (Jari Litmanen for Liverpool).
Delighted in a club record Stadium of Light crowd of 48,285 (v. Leeds United).
Staged a UEFA International Final – France 0–1 Spain – and welcomed the President of UEFA to Wearside.
Saw Darren Williams, Niall Quinn and Kevin Phillips play their 150th competitive game for the club.

Peter Reid managed his 250th league game for Sunderland AFC (v. Aston Villa).

Peter Reid managed his 300th competitive game (v. Newcastle United).

DELL HELL!

From 1964 to 1996 Sunderland made 15 league trips to The Dell and **NEVER WON A SOLITARY GAME** against Southampton, drawing four and losing eleven.

LONG LIVE THE QUEEN!

In 1977 and to celebrate Queen Elizabeth II's Silver Jubilee, Sunderland's away strip was red, white and blue. It became affectionately known as 'The Jubilee Strip'.

WE OWE IT TO THE SCOTS

In October 1879 Sunderland & District Teachers' Association was founded by a man from Ayrshire, James Allen. In time the football club became known quite simply as Sunderland AFC.

In the early days the football club recruited the majority of its players from Scotland. The Scots, at that time, were widely regarded as the best footballers in the world. As proof of this, Sunderland's victory over Hearts on a trip to Tynecastle in the late nineteenth century resulted not only in a red and white victory, but the crown of World Champions.

The last time Sunderland AFC won the English league title, their captain was a Scot, Alex Hastings. Our last domestic trophy, the FA Cup won in 1973, was held aloft by our then skipper Bobby Kerr, also a Scotsman. In 1937 our very first FA Cup triumph, in defeating Preston North End, was accomplished with a Scottish manager, Johnny Cochrane, formerly of St Mirren, at the helm.

Our entry into league football was due in no small part to a Scotsman, William McGregor, the Football League's founder, who, after witnessing Sunderland's 7–2 demolition of Aston Villa in April 1890, indicated that Sunderland 'had a talented man in every position'. The legend of the Team Of All The Talents was born and Wearside witnessed professional football just a few months later.

SING WHEN YOU'RE WINNING?

Sunderland AFC have played in 108 competitive league seasons. The following are the crowd averages in descending average order. It clearly demonstrates two boom times for Association Football in England; the years after the end of the Second World War up to the late 1950s, and the seasons from the late 1990s and the growing popularity of the Premier League. Out of Sunderland's top 25 averages, only 4 seasons don't fall within the aforementioned periods.

Average Crowds

Season	Games	Average	Aggregate
1949/50	21	47,785	1,003,485
2000/01	19	46,832	889,800
2001/02	19	46,745	888,156
1948/49	21	45,220	949,620
2007/08	19	43,344	823,540
1954/55	21	43,043	903,903
1947/48	21	42,888	900,648
1953/54	21	42,505	892,605
1999/2000	19	41,375	786,133
1963/64	21	41,258	866,418
1962/63	21	40,883	858,543
1964/65	21	40,637	853,377
2008/09	19	40,168	763,198
1951/52	21	39,853	836,913
1952/53	21	39,767	835,107
1950/51	21	39,766	835,086
2002/03	19	39,698	754,267
1998/99	23	38,745	891,133

Season	Games	Average	Aggregate
1957/58	21	36,146	759,066
1956/57	21	36,145	759,045
1955/56	21	35,888	753,648
1946/47	21	35,301	741,321
1997/98	23	34,523	794,029
1965/66	21	34,488	724,248
2005/06	19	33,904	644,180
1961/62	21	32,986	692,706
1976/77	21	32,743	687,603
2006/07	23	31,887	733,406
1966/67	21	31,731	666,351
1975/76	21	31,250	656,250
1967/68	21	30,873	648,333
1935/36	21	30,378	637,938
1974/75	21	29,931	628,551
2004/05	23	28,821	662,874
1920/21	21	28,765	604,065
1936/37	21	28,670	602,070
1958/59	21	27,772	583,212
2003/04	23	27,127	623,921
1979/80	21	27,119	569,499
1980/81	21	26,477	556,017
1960/61	21	26,051	547,071
1919/20	21	25,580	537,180
1978/79	21	25,454	534,534
1968/69	21	25,426	533,946
1934/35	21	25,397	533,337
1928/29	21	25,196	529,116
1937/38	21	25,132	527,772
1929/30	21	24,553	515,613
1973/74	21	24,409	512,589
1921/22	21	24,150	507,150
1923/24	21	23,475	492,975
1931/32	21	23,131	485,751
1922/23	21	23,070	484,470
1959/60	21	22,831	479,451
1972/73	21	22,603	474,663
1990/91	19	22,577	428,963
1977/78	21	22,276	467,796

Season	Games	Average	Aggregate
1930/31	21	22,015	462,315
1969/70	21	21,790	457,590
1938/39	21	21,470	450,870
1927/28	21	21,411	449,631
1925/26	21	21,399	449,379
1913/14	19	20,865	396,435
1996/97	19	20,865	396,435
1924/25	21	20,440	429,240
1981/82	21	19,608	411,768
1991/92	23	18,390	422,970
1984/85	21	18,347	385,287
1933/34	21	18,269	383,649
1926/27	21	18,142	380,982
1989/90	23	17,987	413,701
1912/13	19	17,940	340,860
1995/96	23	17,482	402,086
1907/08	19	17,470	331,930
1987/88	23	17,425	400,775
1982/83	21	17,370	364,770
1992/93	23	17,258	396,934
1932/33	21	17,254	362,334
1993/94	23	16,934	389,482
1910/11	19	16,650	316,350
1983/84	21	16,180	339,780
1985/86	21	16,052	337,092
1971/72	21	15,906	334,026
1970/71	21	15,780	331,380
1906/07	19	15,450	293,550
1994/95	23	15,344	352,912
1902/03	17	15,305	260,185
1908/09	19	15,235	289,465
1988/89	23	14,878	342,194
1904/05	17	14,510	246,670
1903/04	17	13,670	232,390
1986/87	21	13,601	285,621
1905/06	19	13,015	247,285
1911/12	19	12,555	238,545
1898/99	17	12,540	213,180
1901/02	17	12,095	205,615

Season	Games	Average	Aggregate
1900/01	17	11,695	198,815
1909/10	19	11,615	220,685
1899/00	17	11,265	191,505
1897/98	15	10,970	164,550
1914/15	19	10,230	194,370
1894/95	15	8,250	123,750
1891/92	13	8,225	106,925
1892/93	15	7,815	117,225
1893/94	15	6,890	103,350
1895/96	15	6,210	93,150
1890/91	11	5,950	65,450
1896/97	15	5,160	77,400
Totals	2,174	24,957	54,255,480

OLD BUT GOLD

Joe Kasher, born in Willington, County Durham, died at Middlesbrough on 8 January 1992 just days short of his ninety-eighth birthday. A life-long friend of goalscoring legend Charlie Buchan, it is almost certain that he was Sunderland AFC's longest-surviving player. Kasher served in the First World War and was thrilled in May 1919 to sign for the team he had supported since he was a boy. He was a centre-half who played 89 times for the red and whites. At the time of his death it was rumoured that he was also English football's oldest ex-professional player.

It is likely that Sunderland AFC's first-born league footballer was Johnny Auld who played 116 times for the Black Cats. He was born on 7 January 1862.

DID YOU KNOW?

On 15 November 1936, Sunderland went to France to play Nord FC. The game was watched by the French Minister for Sport.

King Farouk of Egypt watched Sunderland win the 1937 FA Cup Final against Preston North End at Wembley Stadium.

On 28 November 1884, Sunderland travelled to Castle Eden, where they triumphed 4–1 against the home side. The match was played over two periods of 25 minutes.

In seasons 1884/85 and 1887/88, Sunderland conceded eleven goals in single matches against Scottish opponents; Port Glasgow & Cambuslang.

On 26 December 1889, Sunderland defeated the Welsh Champions, Druids, 12–0.

In August and September of 1891 the Canadian touring team played four games against Third Lanark, Kings Park, Linfield Athletic and Sunderland. The tourists lost every game!

SUNDERLAND DRAW THE CROWDS

Over the years, Sunderland have proved to be a big attraction for other clubs, be it due to their large travelling support, the occasion, the regard with which the club is held or simply because they were a team recognised for playing good football as proven by:

Leeds United's record crowd is 57,892 at Elland Road versus Sunderland in a 1967 FA Cup replay.

On 5 March 1938, Spurs' record crowd of 75,038 spectators witnessed the team lose by a single goal to Sunderland.

The record attendance for an Arsenal match at Highbury is 73,295 for a 0–0 draw against Sunderland on 9 March 1935.

MISSING TROPHY

The first trophy ever won by Sunderland AFC was as an amateur side in 1884, the Durham Association Challenge Cup. However, as the Durham Football Association did not have enough money, no actual trophy was won. In fact the medals awarded to the players were not presented to the side until 6 July, some two months after the game. The trophy was won again in 1887, this time both a trophy and medals were awarded at the appropriate time!

MERRY CHRISTMAS!

The last time SAFC played a match on Christmas Day was the 1956 clash with Aston Villa in which the Black Cats won 1–0.

Sunderland have played 31 league games on Christmas Day, 19 away and 12 at home, winning 13, losing 12 with 6 draws.

The best Christmas Day sequence of results was from 1909 to 1914 where Sunderland won 5 consecutive matches.

Conversely, from 1919 to 1936 Sunderland lost 8 out of 9 fixtures played on Christmas Day, drawing the other.

THE STADIUM OF LIGHT: THE BIGGEST PUB IN THE COUNTRY?

When Scottish & Newcastle (S&N) won the pouring rights to the Stadium of Light, it was on the condition that rival breweries couldn't sell their products until a certain volume of alcohol had been consumed by the fans. Initial estimates indicated that it would take perhaps three years for the club to sell the required amount.

After one season the whole agreement lay in tatters and Vaux Breweries were then allowed in as well as S&N. Not that the former Newcastle-based brewing giants were complaining; with some 50,000 pints sold at every home game this surely made the Sunderland Stadium of Light the biggest pub in the country!

THEY SAID IT...

'We could win and I could be sacked. I could lose and be sacked.'

Sunderland manager Ricky Sbragia reflects on his position after the 3–1 defeat by Portsmouth that left the club teetering on the brink of a 2008/09 relegation

'These are my people; you cannot treat them like that.'

Chairman Niall Quinn indicates to a member of Easyjet's staff at Cardiff airport what his position is after celebrating Sunderland fans were made to leave the plane at Bristol Airport following a victory at Cardiff City. Quinn subsequently paid for taxis to take the fans home to Sunderland

'I learned my trade at Arsenal, became a footballer at Manchester City, but Sunderland got under my skin; I love Sunderland.'

Niall Quinn becomes the latest member of the Roker Roar following this admission in his autobiography

SUNDERLAND'S FIRST RIVALRY

Curiously, Sunderland's first great rivalry in football wasn't strictly with Newcastle United. Before that battle could commence in earnest, Sunderland AFC had to see off the threat posed by another team in the then town; Sunderland Albion, who had been formed by James Allan, the founder of Sunderland AFC. Although Albion would subsequently fold in the early 1890s due to financial difficulties, it was not before bitterness and acrimony between the two clubs.

This was never better demonstrated than the game between the two on 12 January 1889. With Sunderland AFC refusing to go to Hendon for a game at Albion's home venue, Newcastle Road (Sunderland's then stadium) saw 10,000 pack in to witness a what would become a very violent affair. Twenty policemen were on duty in case of crowd trouble and at 2.20 p.m. the game kicked off.

Albion raced into a two-goal lead, but Sunderland fought back to equalise. With minutes remaining Sunderland scored again. However, the goal was so hotly disputed (over the crossbar – remember no nets in those days) that the Albion players left the field in a fit of pique. All hell broke loose and Albion's transport was stoned in North Bridge Street.

James Allan sustained a nasty eye injury that required surgery, which was ironic considering that the gate receipts were being donated to the Children's Hospital, Eye Infirmary, Infirmary and Monkwearmouth dispensary.

Dr Norman Davis attended to James Allan at his surgery, and such was the severity of the incident that all Albion players were interviewed by the police after the game at the Waverley Hotel. The Albion players were adamant that they would never again play at the Newcastle Road ground, and there was universal condemnation of the treatment they had received by the Sunderland fans.

TIMELINE:
THE STADIUM OF LIGHT

11 December 1996 – it became evident that the original planned stadium capacity of 34,000 had been a gross underestimate and Sunderland chairman Bob Murray revealed that Sunderland intended to seek permission for a 40,040 capacity at their new Wearmouth stadium. The decision to increase capacity was taken after consultation with the stadium's funding partners who had taken into account existing planning approval, set for 29,000 initially, increasing to 34,000.

23 February 1996 – the tenders for the Sunderland AFC super-stadium were opened at the Football Trust offices in London at 2 p.m. The club received three formal tenders for the construction of the stadium and the companies selected to tender were:

1.   Ballast Nedam – who were involved in the building of Holland and Ajax of Amsterdam's new stadium.

2. Birse – whose current stadium experience included the construction of the £18m, 25,000-seater stand for Manchester United.
3. Taylor Woodrow – whose recent work had included development of Middlesbrough's then new Riverside Stadium.

27 March 1996 – the Board of Sunderland AFC selected Ballast Wiltshier plc, part of the leading international construction group Ballast Nedam NV, as the main contractor for its all-seater stadium at the former Wearmouth Colliery site in Sunderland.

26 April 1996 – the Board of Sunderland AFC gave construction company Ballast Wiltshier the green light to begin work on their new £15 million 40,000-seat stadium at a press conference on Thursday 25 April 1996. Ballast Wiltshier were scheduled to begin work on the stadium on Wednesday 15 May 1996.

11 February 1997 – Sunderland AFC announced that it had started to install the first seats at the club's new super stadium. All the seats within the stadium were to be Sunderland red in colour, with the exception of those where an image or lettering appeared.

17 March 1997 – Sunderland revealed that it would not take up residence in the club's new 42,000-seat stadium in the summer. In an ambitious move, more often associated with Europe's top clubs, Sunderland's commercial hub and ticket office operation was to be located in a purpose-built, state of the art £1 million office complex on Stadium Park. This surprising and innovative decision to locate the club's offices away from the new stadium enabled the club to expand and maximise its first-class business and hospitality facilities within the stadium. It was the latest in a series of positive and unique steps announced by the club. The new 15,000sq ft offices were to be located close to the north-east corner of the stadium, and were designed by stadium architects Taylor Tulip & Hunter to complement the design and finish of the West Stand. With the addition of the club's office development, the total cost of the stadium, car park and fit-out increased from £15 million to £19 million.

25 June 1997 – Sunderland AFC revealed that it had received approval to open the club's new super stadium at full capacity. Tyne and Wear Development Corporation has confirmed that all major planning conditions associated with opening the stadium at full capacity on day one had been discharged by Sunderland AFC.

29 July 1997, Midnight – Sunderland AFC announced the name of their magnificent new stadium – the Sunderland Stadium of Light.

30 July 1997 – The Stadium of Light opened with a friendly against Dutch footballing giants Ajax of Amsterdam. A new chapter opened up in the history of Sunderland AFC.

WEARSIDE WOE:
1992 FA CUP FINAL

Sunderland 0–2 Liverpool, 9 May 1992, Wembley

This was the fourth time Liverpool and Sunderland had met in the FA Cup, with the Merseysiders just shading it 2–0. In 1921/22 the teams had played out a 1–1 draw, with Liverpool winning the replay 5–0. In 1960/61 Sunderland won a fourth-round tie at Anfield 2–0, and in 1981/82 Liverpool had won 3–0 at Roker Park.

For Liverpool's tenth final and Sunderland's fourth, the Scousers were the overwhelming favourites; the Wearsiders were a division below.

In the 111th FA Cup Final, John Byrne was trying to join a small band of players who had scored in every round, and in the first half he had a glorious chance, but luck would desert him that day. Bracewell also had a good shot, but deflected just wide and one began to get the impression that this wasn't to be their day; and so it proved.

Second half and even the double-banking of McManaman by Rogan and Armstrong couldn't prevent Liverpool running riot, and it came as no surprise when a spectacular effort by Michael Thomas put the Merseysiders one up, and firmly in the driving seat. Ian Rush (who else?) added a second with twenty-four minutes remaining.

There was no disgrace for Sunderland, who had put up a great show, but in the end were quite simply beaten by the better team on the day. It was an ideal present for Liverpool manager Graeme Souness who had just come out of hospital after heart bypass surgery.

Sunderland were greeted home by tens of thousands of people, who acknowledged once more that the team had nearly triumphed against all the odds.

Sunderland: Norman, Owers, Ball, Bennett, Rogan, Rush (Hardyman), Bracewell, Davenport, Armstrong, Byrne, Atkinson (Hawke).
Liverpool: Grobbelaar, Jones, Burrows, Nicol, Molby, Wright, Saunders, Houghton, Rush, McManaman, Thomas.

Referee: Mr Philip Don (Middlesex) Attendance: 79,554

STOKOE WONDERLAND:
1973 FA CUP FINAL

Leeds United 0–1, Sunderland, 5 May 1973, Wembley

In the run up to the 1973 final there was, as predicted, a huge scramble for tickets, with the lucky few getting hold of them in London on the day of the match. For the rest of the non-season ticket holders, there was the prospect of a ballot draw from the forms issued at the Carlisle United and Bristol City home games.

Sunderland spent the days before the final at the Selsdon Park Hotel in Surrey where they sized up the formidable opposition they were about to face. Predictably, Leeds United were quoted at 3-1 on to win the final with Sunderland at 5-2.

Sunderland's youth team were hoping to get the week off to a good start but they succumbed to defeat by Middlesbrough in the two-legged Northern Intermediate League Cup Final. Trailing 5–4 on aggregate, Jackie Ashurst had the chance to draw level with a penalty, but blazed the ball over the bar.

For Bob Stokoe the cup final would be his sixteenth cup tie of the season, seven with his former club Blackpool. The Sunderland team would be the same as the semi-final, bar the substitute. With Brian Chambers now an Arsenal player, David Young would be the twelfth man for Sunderland.

In Scotland that year, the Cup Final was contested by Rangers and Celtic. The 'Gers triumphed 3–2 in front of 122,000 (the last of such big crowds in Scotland) with the winning goal scored by Tam Forsyth.

In England the FA Cup Final took place on 5 May 1973. In years to come the question for every Sunderland fans was, 'where were you at 3:31 p.m.?' With the President of the Football Association, HRH the Duke of Kent, in attendance, Wearside took on the might of Yorkshire and Leeds United. Quite simply, the Peacocks were a 'football machine' and were one of the most feared sides in Europe, with an international competing for every place. They had come a long way since their promotion in 1964.

Oddly enough, the two managers found themselves on opposing sides again with Don Revie and Bob Stokoe having contested the 1955 Final when Newcastle United took on Manchester City. Sunderland had played Leeds United before in the FA Cup in 1926/27 and a three-match marathon in 1967, all won by the Yorkshire side. In the run up to the final Sunderland had used seventeen players.

In the twenty days before Wembley, Sunderland played eight league games, giving them a return, since Bob Stokoe took over, of 30 points from 22 games – promotion standard. The nation had taken Sunderland to their hearts; and the boys did not disappoint. They were without awe of Leeds; they chased them, they looked for goals.

Bobby Kerr won the toss for Sunderland and elected to defend the end where the Leeds United fans had massed. As if to prove the lack of fear on the part of Sunderland, Ritchie Pitt scythed down Allan Clarke early on. Reputations counted for nothing in this game.

After half an hour, Harvey in the Leeds goal lifted a lob from Kerr over the bar. The corner from Hughes was sent back into the centre by Halom, and Porterfield, bringing the ball down with his left thigh, turned a little and hit it hard with his right into the net.

Montgomery's famous double save was in the second half when Jones switched play to Reaney on the right. Reaney's high cross to the far post was met by Cherry with a diving header which Montgomery, lunging himself to the left, knocked out, but only to Lorimer on the six-yard line. Lorimer hit it quickly and cleanly into the apparently empty space on the other side of the goalkeeper. Montgomery managed to throw himself that way and jerk the ball upwards with his right arm. It struck the underside of the bar and came out wide and Malone thumped it miles away.

It was now believable that Sunderland could win. Leeds built up attack after attack, but Sunderland's rear four were commanding. Every clearance was cheered. For some the tension was unbearable and they left their seats and paced about under the stands, while at home others had to leave their TVs.

Everyone except the unfortunate folk from Leeds wanted the final whistle to blow and when it did there was one of the greatest roars ever at Wembley. Bob Stokoe, his short white mackintosh billowing, raced across to Montgomery.

Danny Blanchflower wrote that the game was the most emotional he had known. The *Sunday Express* said Wembley had never seen such ecstasy; the nation enthused. Back in Sunderland many people ran out; there was impromptu dancing; cars appeared, drivers just sounding their horns. The centre of the town became impassable. That night was just about the most joyous the old town had known. Don Revie, who took defeat well, said that Montgomery's save was the best he had seen, and that Sunderland's strength and enthusiasm in the first half had unsettled his side.

Leeds United: Harvey, Reaney, Cherry, Bremner, Madeley, Hunter, Lorimer, Clarke, Jones, Giles, Gray (Yorath)

Sunderland: Montgomery, Malone, Guthrie, Horswill, Pitt, Halom, Hughes, Kerr, Watson, Porterfield, Tueart

Referee: Ken Burns (Stourbridge) Attendance: 100,000

SACKED AFTER A POOLS PANEL DEFEAT!

Malcolm Crosby was Sunderland's manager during the 1991/92 and 1992/93 seasons, enduring an eventful 277-day tenure during which he took Sunderland AFC to the 1992 FA Cup Final. However, the manner of his dismissal was bizarre, even by Sunderland AFC standards.

Crosby, who stood on the Wembley terraces as a Sunderland fan at the 1973 FA Cup Final, left Sunderland seventeenth in the First Division – exactly their position when he had replaced Denis Smith on a caretaker basis thirteen months earlier. Ironically, Smith was sacked by Bristol City a fortnight before Crosby at Sunderland.

Clamour for Crosby's appointment to be made permanent grew as Sunderland advanced on Wembley, where they eventually lost to Liverpool. However, when the board's offer of a contract came, it was for one year only.

Nevertheless, Crosby was taken aback by the timing of his demise after a game at Tranmere Rovers was postponed, making him probably the first manager to be ousted after a Pools Panel defeat. The latter had predicted a home win. Only at Sunderland could this happen!

MACHINE-GUNNED
WATCHING SUNDERLAND!

On 30 May 1942 Sunderland AFC made a trip to the Midlands to play Wolverhampton Wanderers in the 1942 War Cup final, which was a regional substitute for the FA Cup during the Second World War.

A North-East newspaper reported the following:

> Sunderland supporters on their way to Wolverhampton for the [War] Cup Final had the experience of being under machine gun fire from the air in the early hours of Saturday morning. Between 60 and 70 Wearsiders were passengers on a train which it is thought was the target of a Nazi hit-and-run raider which swooped on

the station of a North-East town . . . bullets were heard splattering on the station roof and on the track; no one was injured and the train continued on its journey.

The passengers reckoned that the plane was no more than 100ft from the ground. Due to reporting restrictions the name of the railway station was not allowed to be published, however locals knew it was Newcastle Central station.

Puts a whole new slant on precarious trips to Millwall!

END OF AN ERA

After 99 years Sunderland AFC left their home, Roker Park, in 1997. The facts and figures surrounding their tenure at the famous old stadium tells its own tale:

First goal	Jimmy Leslie v. Liverpool, 10 September 1898
Last league goal	Allan Johnston v. Everton, 3 May 1997
Last competitive goal	Paul Beavers v. Middlesbrough (Northern Intermediate League), 7 May 1997
Last ever goal	John Mullin v. Liverpool, 13 May 1997
Highest crowd	75,118 v. Derby County, March 1933
Highest league crowd	68,004 v. Newcastle United, March 1950
Lowest crowd	3,841 v. Manchester City, April 1934
Highest scoring match	England 13–2 Ireland, February 1899 (Ground Record)
Highest scoring match	Sunderland 8–2 Blackburn Rovers, February 1931
Biggest Sunderland victory	Sunderland 8–1 Charlton Ath, September 1956 (League)

Biggest Sunderland victory	Sunderland 9–0 Chatham, January 1914 (FA Cup)
Total league games	1812
	996 wins
	449 draws
	367 defeats

BOMB DAMAGE!

When German bombs fell in Sunderland and along the north-east coast on 16 and 24 May 1943, after a lull of a few months, no less than 55 of the 223 fatalities were children under sixteen years of age. Many of the town's children though, had long since been evacuated to places such as Leyburn in the Yorkshire Dales. All in all, some 52,494 children were evacuated from Newcastle, Sunderland and the surrounding areas. Only London, Merseyside and Manchester had more child evacuees, which demonstrates how integrated heavy industry (and potential bombing targets) was in the north-east.

On the night of 15 May and early hours of 16 May, Sunderland suffered at the hands of the Luftwaffe and a German bombing raid that saw a device land on Roker Park, entering through the Main Stand roof, leaving a large crater in the playing surface.

Just two months later, another bomb fell outside the ground near the Roker End, killing Special Constable Lancelot Slawther as he patrolled near his home in Beatrice Street. The bomb also destroyed the Club House at the corner of the Roker End and the Main Stand. The close proximity of the football ground to the shipyards meant that it was bound to be hit sooner or later.

SUNDERLAND CHANGE THEIR NAME!

Following the 1966 FIFA World Cup being held in England and broadcast in the United States, promoters came together to start up two professional soccer leagues in USA – the United

Soccer Association (sanctioned by FIFA and the United States Soccer Federation) and the National Professional Soccer League (not sanctioned).

The reason for the formation was clear – the World Cup had been won, for the first time, by an English-speaking nation and television audiences for the competition had been high in the USA. The game was further promoted in the USA by the documentary film *Goal!* which was the official FIFA film of the 1966 tournament. Never short of entrepreneurs, various businessmen, particularly stadium owners, saw the potential for a rebirth of the sport in their country.

With encouragement and sanctioning from the United States Soccer Federation and FIFA, the North American Soccer League (NASL) in 1967 announced plans to begin operating in 1968.

Suddenly confronted by a competitor, the National Professional Soccer League (NPSL), the NASL changed its name to the United Soccer Association (USA) to avoid confusion with the other league and decided to play its first season in 1967.

Owing to a distinct lack of time for recruiting their own players to teams, the United Soccer Association imported full teams from other nations, placing them in US and Canadian cities, thus forming outfits for a summer league (summer season represented the off-season for European and South American leagues).

In Europe the tournament was allegedly brokered by the TV commentator Kenneth Wolstenholme, former England forward Jimmy Greaves, ex-Nottingham Forest forward Roy Dwight (an uncle of Elton John) and London businessman Jim Graham.

Among the rival NPSL's backers were Art Rooney, owner of the NFL's Pittsburgh Steelers, and Jerry Hoffberger, owner of baseball's Baltimore Orioles.

It had ten teams: the Atlanta Chiefs, Baltimore Bays, California Clippers, Chicago Spurs, Los Angles Toros, New York Generals, Philadelphia Spartans, Pittsburgh Phantoms, St Louis Stars and Toronto Falcons. Because the NPSL was not sanctioned by soccer's national and international governing bodies, as the USA was, its teams had problems finding players, since they faced possible suspension for playing in the league.

Sunderland AFC, as part of the United Soccer Association, became the Vancouver Royal Canadians; Brazil's Bangu Atlético Clube, among others, became the Houston Stars. Together they joined a further ten original teams in the United Soccer Association.

The other international teams were: Scottish clubs Dundee United (Dallas Tornado), Hibernian (Toronto City), Aberdeen (Washington Whips), English clubs Wolverhampton Wanderers (Los Angeles Wolves), Stoke City (Cleveland Stokers), Uruguay's Cerro Porteno (New York Skyliners), Holland's ADO Den Haag (San Francisco Golden Gate Gales), Northern Ireland's Glentoran of Belfast (Detroit Cougars), Italy's Cagliari (Chicago Mustangs) and Ireland's Shamrock Rovers (Boston Rovers).

The twelve-game season began in late May 1967 and ran through to mid-July, with Los Angeles defeating the Washington Whips 6–5 in extra time in the first Championship game.

In April 1967, the ten-team National Professional Soccer League also kicked off with a thirty-two-game schedule. The Oakland Clippers defeated the Baltimore Rays in a two-game championship series.

In December of 1967, the two leagues (the United Soccer Association and National Professional Soccer League) merged and seventeen of the twenty-two teams remained to form the North American Soccer League (NASL) – which remained the top US soccer league until 1984. The NASL would, of course, become synonymous with star footballers such as George Best, Franz Beckenbauer and the incomparable, legendary, Pelé.

Today it is known as the MLS (Major League Soccer) and Sunderland, as the Vancouver Royal Canadians, were pioneers of it!

SUNDERLAND AFC MAJOR HONOURS
1879 TO 1939

	Champions/ Winners	Runners-Up/ Finalists
Football League 1	1891/92, 1892/93, 1894/95, 1901/02, 1912/13, 1935/36	1893/94, 1897/98, 1900/01, 1922/23, 1934/35
FA Cup	1936/37	1912/13
Charity Shield/ Sheriff of London Shield	1902/03, 1936/37	1937/38

SUNDERLAND:
THE BEST TEAM IN THE LAND

There is Doig in goal with Porteous
And Donald Gow the famous back
Wilson, Auld and Murray,
At half back are the cracks
The two Hannahs, Campbell, Miller and Scott,
As forwards they are grand
Play up, good old Sunderland,
The best team in the land

**Ode sung by Sunderland supporters in tribute to
The Team Of All The Talents in 1892 to the tune of
'Maggie Murphy's Home'**

SUNDERLAND TRAINER LAYS OUT
OPPOSITION FAN!

John Grayston, a founder member of Sunderland AFC in 1879, recalls how Sunderland had an early trainer who was a boxer/ fighter, who put the team in 'good form' and accompanied the team on visits to opponents' grounds. 'He was a useful supporter, and laid out one man at Newcastle who very unwisely interfered with one of our backs.'

GROUND-BREAKING FIRSTS

Sunderland of course played at other home venues before settling at Roker Park and then the Stadium of Light. Here are some facts about the firsts associated with the club's former homes:

The game against Ferryhill on 13 November 1880 was Sunderland's first game at Blue House Field.

The game against The Rangers on 12 February 1881 was played at St James' Park, clearly marking Sunderland down as having played at the ground before Newcastle United took up tenancy. Stanley Cricket club, from South Byker, who would become Newcastle East End and join with West End to ultimately become Newcastle United, were not formed until November 1881.

From the Blue House Field, Sunderland moved to Percy Terrace and then 'to another field', before ending up at The Grove (Groves Field), near Ashbrooke. However, on 11 February 1882, Sunderland played North Eastern, but at Whitburn Cricket Club, so we therefore look to have another ground to add to the list.

The game against North Eastern on 4 November 1882 was Sunderland's first game at Groves Field.

The game against Castle Eden on 29 September 1883 was Sunderland's first game at Horatio Street – the 'Clay-Dolly' field.

The game against Birtley on 27 September 1884 was Sunderland's first game at Abbs Field, Fulwell, near the old Blue House Inn.

The game against Birtley on 10 April 1886 was Sunderland's first game at Newcastle Road.

OPPOSITION GOALKEEPER LOSES THE PLOT!

Castle Eden were regular opponents for Sunderland AFC in the early days of the club and on one occasion Sunderland players gave their goalkeeper a rough ride. When he had been thrown to the mud for the third time in the match, he threatened revenge and rushed out at one of the Sunderland players to inflict harm on him. However, as he chased after the player, Sunderland's founder James Allan scored in the vacant net! The goalkeeper later apologised for his actions.

THE PRINCE OF GOALKEEPERS

Sunderland's very first league victory came again West Bromwich Albion, 20 September 1890, at Stoney Lane, a 4–0 triumph that witnessed the debut of John Edward 'Teddy' Doig in the Sunderland goal. He had been transferred from Arbroath and was known as the 'Prince of Goalkeepers'. Doig had been a witness to the Scottish club's 36–0 slaughter of Bon Accord in the first round of the Scottish Cup on 5 September 1885, still a world record score, and had played for them as early as 1883.

At that time players were paid a maximum wage of 25 shillings per week during the season, and 10 shillings per week out of season, so they also needed jobs. Most Sunderland players got employment with either the Manor Quay or North Sands shipyard, while some took jobs at Dickinson's Engine Works.

Doig was given a job in the North Sands shipyard office and in time would be a magnificent servant to Sunderland. He had a bald head and covered it, always, with a cap, held in place by a piece of elastic under his chin! In one famous incident, a match against Glasgow Celtic, his cap blew off and he is alleged to have raced around the penalty area to retrieve it, rather than the ball! He was quite a character. Not only that, he was quite a goalkeeper, and Sunderland were beaten only once at home in 6 seasons (82 home games) after his arrival. Doig lived at Forster Street, off Roker Avenue.

His transfer was, however, not without its controversy. While playing for Arbroath he was induced to sign for Blackburn Rovers and played a trial match for them against Notts County. He was subsequently suspended by the Scottish Football Association and signed for Sunderland once his suspension had expired. In effect he was on the books of two clubs (he was still registered with Blackburn). This resulted in a 2 point penalty and a £50 fine for Sunderland AFC. Not the greatest of starts to life in the Football League.

THE PENALTY THAT NEVER WAS

On 28 February 1891, Sunderland played Notts County at Bramall Lane in the semi-final of the FA Cup. It was the red and whites' first such occasion and the game was marked by untold drama. First of all, Sunderland had a Johnny Campbell effort disallowed after three minutes for offside. Notts County then took the lead and an own goal pegged the score back. Harvie then gave Sunderland a shock lead before the pendulum once more swung in County's favour before half time.

In the second half the Nottingham team gained a curious advantage when they claimed that a shot had gone in off the underside of the crossbar. Owing to the fact that nets wouldn't be used until the following season, they were of course referring to the 'chord'. The referee inexplicably gave the goal. To Sunderland's credit they fought back and goalscorer par excellence Johnny Campbell gained a well-deserved draw and a replay.

In a bizarre twist of fate, in the replay the County team were incensed when Porteous handled the ball in the box, when it was clearly travelling into the net. Notwithstanding the fact that the Sunderland goalkeeper was Doig, the penalty-kick had not yet been introduced (as 'gentlemen' were not supposed to do anything other than play to the rules), and so this was viewed very dimly by the crowd who made their feelings known in no uncertain terms. Porteous went unpunished. The penalty-kick was not introduced until the 1891/92 season.

RAINING GOALS

Sunderland won their second championship in the 1892/93 season, and in doing so became the first team to score 100 goals in a single league season. This was also the initial season of the 'First Division'. The 100 goal record would remain until 1919/20 when West Bromwich Albion surpassed the total – playing 12 games more.

By the end of the 1892/93 season, Sunderland had played 59 games, winning 45, losing 9 and drawing 5. They scored 199 goals and conceded just 68.

In two years Sunderland amassed over 400 goals and lost just 18 out of 117 games.

HUGH THROWS THE GAME

Captured by Samuel Tyzack from Newmilns, Ayrshire, it is doubtful whether, at his peak, there was a more famous player in the United Kingdom than Hugh Wilson. He was regarded as the greatest half-back Sunderland ever possessed, before he was transferred to Bristol City, eventually making it back home to his native Scotland and Third Lanark. But it was on Wearside that he became famous, in a nine-year red and white career, of nearly 260 appearances.

He started his career at half-back, but in time became a forward and scored some 45 goals for the club. He was a very large man and dominated the Sunderland team, an outfit that was Scottish in all but name, and had a massive throw in. His main strength, though, lay in his powers of perception and anticipation that had more than one opposing forward cursing in frustration. He had an almost telepathic understanding with Johnny Campbell and used his massive kick to great effect, planting long passes perfectly into his fellow Scotsman's path.

That he would in time make the transfer to centre-forward was no surprise, and is probably the earliest exponent of what would become total football; he was at home in any position. On one occasion he even took over from an injured Sunderland goalkeeper, and typically didn't concede.

Due to the length of his one handed throws he was instrumental in having the throw-in rule changed in football where of course it is now a two handed throw.

THE FIRST BACKHANDER?

While the majority of the game was amateur in the 1890s, Sunderland were one of 28 clubs who supported professionalism. Many Lancashire teams were paying Scots and finding them jobs. Such a case was that of Jimmy Hunter. Having been impressed with him in the game against Dumfries, he was signed for Sunderland and was fixed up in the JL Thompson shipyards. This may well have been one of the first 'backhander' payments ever given. Hunter was, in effect, Sunderland's first 'professional' player.

SHIRT SWAP

On 5 March 1898, Sunderland took on Sheffield United at Newcastle Road. While the 3–1 victory was not surprising, there was an interesting incident in the game. The Blades turned up at Sunderland with their customary red and whites shirts; Sunderland played in white shirts that day. By half time the United strips were so wet through that they were forced to change them. The unfortunate thing was that their reserve tops of all white would have clashed with Sunderland's, so Sunderland lent them their red and white shirts in a gesture much appreciated by the Yorkshire team.

ENGLAND'S ROKER PARK RECORD

On 18 February 1899, Roker Park was awarded the England v. Northern Ireland international fixture. Sunderland's Phil Bach was capped by the host nation. On the same day, Sunderland had an away game at Sheffield Wednesday. Andy McCombie replaced Bach at right-back; the latter lost his place and would eventually move to Sheffield United. Bach would eventually become Middlesbrough chairman and an England selector. England won the match 13–2. The score remains an England record to this day.

FOOTBALL'S FIRST
£1,000 PLAYER

Alf Common was born at Millfield in Sunderland and played local football for nearby Jarrow and South Hylton. He signed for his home-town club in 1900, and was sold to Sheffield United in 1901 for £325 where he scored in the 1902 FA Cup Final for the Blades against Southampton at the Crystal Palace. He was then re-signed by the Black Cats for £520, a world record, in June 1904.

He played few games for Sunderland second time around and was eventually transferred to Middlesbrough for the first four-figure transfer fee in football.

Common played his first game for Middlesbrough on 25 February 1905 in a game at Sheffield United and scored the only goal for the Teessiders, a penalty, in a 1–0 win.

Alf Common moved onto Woolwich Arsenal and Preston North End before hanging up his boots in 1914. He died on 3 April 1946 at the age of sixty-five in Darlington, County Durham, where he had run a pub in the town.

ROKER PARK FACTS

Roker Park was originally leased, but became the outright property of Sunderland AFC in 1908.

Sunderland's match at home to Huddersfield Town, scheduled for Christmas Day 1925, was called off due to a frost-bound pitch. There would be no more postponements at Roker Park for thirty-six years (until Charlton Athletic in December 1961).

Ground improvements in 1929 nearly bankrupted the football club and at a meeting of the directors in 1932 they decided to offer the ground for sale to the then Sunderland Corporation for £40,000. The purchase was approved by the council but called off at the eleventh hour after a change of heart by SAFC.

THEY SAID IT ...

'I would not want a great team like Sunderland to score their first goal from a penalty.'
A local referee to Sunderland captain Charlie Thomson during Sunderland's 1913 tour of Hungary on his decision to disregard the Sunderland captain's appeals for a penalty kick

'I am glad to be sent off.'
Charlie Buchan's thoughts on a roughhouse of a match in Berlin during Sunderland's 1913 European tour

STONES MEND BOOTS

During Sunderland's 1913 continental tour, they played a Berlin XI in the German capital. The sole of Roker player Harry Low's boot partially came off during a game, and on asking the home trainer if they had a 'last' in the dressing room to repair them, he said that no one used them. Thus it left Billy Williams, Sunderland's trainer, to repair it with two stones!

SUNDERLAND PLAYER WINS MILITARY MEDAL

During the First World War, Sunderland player Charlie Buchan served with the Grenadier Guards. On being given Lance Corporal status he ended up fighting on the Western Front at the Somme, Cambrai and Passchendaele, three of the bloodiest conflicts of the First World War. That he survived all three to tell the tale is a feat in itself; that he was also decorated for his bravery makes his Boys' Own story complete. They don't make many like Buchan.

In his autobiography, *A Lifetime in Football*, he modestly makes little mention of his war record and the events surrounding his decoration were never revealed. However, here are those details.

Captain in the Grenadier Guards, Buchan's unit was pinned down in battle. In an effort to save his men he stormed a German lookout post with his troops close behind him. They took the lookout post, but in doing so Buchan was bayoneted in the foot by the one German soldier who had remained alive. Luckily for Buchan (a footballer, remember) the bayonet went straight through the gap between his toes. The fate of the German soldier is unknown.

His commendation was made sure when, under enemy fire, he went back to the mess tent to get his men food as their rations had run out. His cause was presumably helped by the fact that he was a fast runner.

Buchan's Military Medal was gazetted on 12 December 1917, won presumably at Cambrai, some 7 miles behind the Hindenburg line, which had been fought the month before. There was no citation with his medal but he was nominated for a commission shortly after he won it.

The Battle at Cambrai is significant in that it was the first time that tanks, some 400 of them, had been used in significant force in a war. To place Buchan's bravery into perspective, the Germans suffered 50,000 casualties and the British 45,000.

The German Army's Chief of Staff, Paul von Hindenburg, described the Battle of Cambrai thus, 'From the point of view, not of scale, but of the obstinacy which the English displayed and the difficulties of the ground for the defenders, the battles which now raged in Flanders put all our battles on the Somme in 1916 completely in the shade.'

SUNDERLAND PLAYER REIGNS IN SPAIN

Tom Thompson was born at Seaham Harbour in 1894. He started his career off at the local Bible Club in 1912/13 before moving onto Seaham Albion in 1913/14. He then served with the RAF during the First World War and was injured following a crash. Following his recovery he was acquired by Sunderland and signed on for the 1919/20 season. He made his debut for Sunderland Reserves against Darlington on 11 October 1919, playing at number 6, left-half. Although he featured a number of times that season for Sunderland's reserves, he left for Gillingham in 1920 and played four seasons for them before moving on to Guildford United. Thompson then signed for Real Murcia in Spain, featuring 11 times for them in 1924/25.

This, perhaps, marks Thompson out as the first player ever to feature on Sunderland's books and then go on to play in mainland Europe for a continental club side. We should also acknowledge Sunderland AFC player Frank Cuggy, who became coach of Celta Vigo in 1923.

UNHELPFUL CROWD

For the cup tie at Leeds on 8 January 1927, the *Sunderland Echo* newspaper reported that 'over 1000 excursionists, bedecked in red and white, travelled from Sunderland. The stand in which they were placed was decorated with streamers and balloons, which also were being thrown around pretty freely. The place, indeed, looked more like a fancy dress carnival than a football grandstand.' Sunderland lost the game. The next week the story was that 'the supporters who went to Leeds and shouted themselves hoarse were more disgusted than dismayed' and 'some of the letters to the Directors and the *Echo* are far from polite and most unhelpful.'

CHAMPAGNE CORK WINS FA CUP FOR SUNDERLAND

Andrew Reid was Sunderland's trainer at the time of the 1937 FA Cup Final, replacing the retired Billy Williams.

Reid was brought to Sunderland by Johnny Cochrane, one year after his appointment, the two of them having been associated at Paisley when Cochrane was with St Mirren. He was 'sounded out' by Cochrane at North Shields Harbour, with Reid on his way to Norway with his Scottish team.

Reid was born in Edinburgh and played most of his twenty-odd professional years as a footballer in the capital and also at Paisley, before becoming trainer at St Mirren, for whom he starred as a full-back. Ironically he had played with Harry Low as a junior, Low being a member of Sunderland's 1912/13 FA Cup Final team.

As with all footballers he was prone to superstition and before the FA Cup tie against Southampton in the 1936/37 run, he was presented with a champagne cork, which he carried all the way to Wembley.

Obviously not enough for Reid, he was presented with a set of brand new Sunderland shirts for the 1937 FA Cup Final. As Sunderland had played in the same shirts all through the earlier cup rounds, Reid disengaged the badge from the new strips and had them sewn onto the old strips that were without a badge. He did not want to tempt fate by discarding the old strips which he thought had brought luck so far in the competition. Sunderland won the 1937 FA Cup Final.

BLACK CAT GOES TO WEMBLEY

Sunderland's 1937 FA Cup triumph was their first in the famous domestic knockout competition. When the dust had settled on the victory it emerged that a young supporter by the name of Billy Morris had got into Wembley Stadium with a black kitten in the inside top pocket of his jacket, put there to bring Sunderland's players good luck against Preston North End.

CLUB BY CLUB

The following is Sunderland AFC's league record against all
clubs they have played for points.

Opponents	W	D	L	Other	F	A
Accrington Stanley	4	1	1	0	22	12
Aldershot	1	0	1	0	5	4
Arsenal	43	35	46	0	181	198
Aston Villa	51	38	65	0	235	247
Barnsley	14	2	8	0	36	27
Birmingham City	48	20	34	0	162	125
Blackburn Rovers	57	24	41	0	211	170
Blackpool	22	16	16	0	81	81
Bolton Wanderers	51	29	46	0	213	182
Bournemouth	3	1	0	0	6	3
Bradford City	16	11	11	0	54	33
Bradford Park Avenue	2	3	1	0	14	9
Brentford	8	3	3	0	28	20
Brighton & Hove	14	7	13	0	51	46
Bristol City	12	13	15	0	51	58
Bristol Rovers	8	8	8	0	48	36
Burnley	39	25	32	0	147	151
Bury	30	8	18	0	102	74
Cambridge United	2	3	3	0	13	15
Cardiff City	19	14	23	0	73	93
Carlisle United	6	3	3	0	20	18
Charlton Athletic	26	20	28	0	117	113
Chelsea	35	20	49	0	151	177
Chester City	1	0	1	0	2	3
Chesterfield	1	1	0	0	4	3
Colchester United	1	0	1	0	4	4
Coventry City	10	12	10	0	32	33
Crewe Alexandra	6	1	1	0	16	7
Crystal Palace	9	9	10	0	20	26
Darwen	4	0	0	0	21	1
Derby County	56	26	46	0	203	181
Doncaster Rovers	2	0	0	0	5	1

Opponents	W	D	L	Other	F	A
Everton	61	22	65	0	242	248
Fulham	20	13	13	0	66	56
Gillingham	4	2	0	0	12	4
Glossop North End	1	1	0	0	2	0
Grimsby Town	27	12	9	0	96	60
Huddersfield Town	35	26	19	0	132	100
Hull City	13	5	10	0	34	30
Ipswich Town	18	7	21	0	58	72
Leeds United	30	16	36	0	114	120
Leicester City	29	19	30	0	106	119
Leyton Orient	13	8	7	0	45	38
Lincoln City	2	2	2	0	9	10
Liverpool	49	31	64	0	210	242
Luton Town	24	9	13	0	82	66
Manchester City	43	19	54	0	176	199
Manchester United	37	26	49	0	174	194
Mansfield Town	4	0	0	0	11	2
Middlesbrough	56	33	39	0	191	163
Millwall	14	7	11	0	51	36
Newcastle United	41	40	49	0	193	200
Northampton Town	3	0	3	0	10	10
Norwich City	11	10	17	0	43	50
Nottingham Forest	36	22	28	0	134	109
Notts County	26	22	26	0	121	104
Oldham Athletic	14	14	12	0	60	54
Oxford United	15	5	6	0	38	20
Peterborough United	3	0	1	0	10	6
Plymouth Argyle	12	4	8	0	44	27
Port Vale	6	7	1	0	22	15
Portsmouth	35	30	31	0	168	147
Preston North End	45	30	31	0	171	153
QPR	10	6	10	0	33	33
Reading	5	3	6	0	18	17
Rotherham United	10	5	3	0	36	13
Scunthorpe United	5	4	3	0	20	15
Sheffield United	57	24	45	0	211	183
Sheffield Wednesday	46	26	40	0	177	172
Shrewsbury Town	6	2	0	0	12	5

Opponents	W	D	L	Other	F	A
Southampton	15	10	21	0	58	64
Southend United	8	0	6	0	25	15
Stockport County	3	1	0	0	7	2
Stoke City	57	28	37	0	179	129
Swansea	9	4	5	0	34	30
Swindon Town	11	6	7	0	41	26
Tottenham Hotspur	34	25	33	0	127	123
Tranmere Rovers	5	2	7	0	17	15
Walsall	5	2	3	0	21	15
Watford	13	13	8	0	64	48
West Brom	56	39	43	0	246	194
West Ham United	26	17	25	0	101	111
Wigan Athletic	3	5	4	0	13	13
Wimbledon	4	2	4	0	11	14
Wolves	44	25	35	0	182	145
Wrexham	3	1	0	0	5	2
York City	5	0	1	0	13	5
Totals	1,768	1,045	1,535	0	6,804	6,194

HENDON'S HERO

It is almost without doubt that Raich Carter was the greatest player ever to wear a red and white shirt. Not only was he a wonderful footballer but he also won the FA Cup for the first time for Sunderland in 1937 and helped his home-town club to capture their last English League championship in 1936.

Carter was born in Hendon, a stone's throw from where Sunderland Football Club was formed. He attended the Hendon Board School as a child, where Sunderland's founder James Allan once taught.

Hendon is traditionally a tough, working-class neighbourhood of Sunderland. When the local authority built a new sports centre in Hendon it was named, fittingly, after Carter. The centre still stands right next to the now school field where Sunderland played its very first home football match in the nineteenth century.

The centre is in pristine condition, no graffiti in sight, maintained and looked after by Carter's own community; a lasting tribute to a fine footballer.

THEY SAID IT ...

'We trained on a diet of a glass of sherry with a raw egg in it because it was supposed to give you energy. And some players would have one before games too.'
Billy Ellis commenting on the Sunderland players' pre-match diet in the 1920s!

'I don't think that the match should ever have started . . . although there would probably have been a riot if the game had been called off.'
Raich Carter remembers the record 75,118 crowd that turned up at Roker Park in 1933 to see the Sunderland v Derby County FA Cup sixth-round replay

'In the dressing room before the game Raich Carter came over to me and said "Don't worry Eddie! Run into an open space and I'll do my best to put the ball in front of you."'
Sunderland winger of the 1930s and '40s Eddie Burbanks recalls the sophisticated tactics of the day

'That is a nice wedding present for you.'
The Queen reminds Raich Carter of his recent marriage as she handed the Sunderland captain the 1937 FA Cup

'When I signed for Sunderland I felt the same as someone who wins the lottery nowadays must feel.'
Sunderland's 1950s left-winger Johnny McSeverney recalls his immediate feelings on signing for the club

'It was a bitterly cold, snowy, sleety day on Wearside; the kind of day when seagulls fly backwards to stop their eyes watering.'
Sunderland's Brian Clough recalls the weather on the day when he was injured against Bury at Roker Park, sustaining knee ligament damage that effectively ended his playing career

'I can remember driving up to Sunderland in my first car, a Ford Consul, and wondering just how far north I had to go. I thought I was driving to the end of the world.'

Charlie Hurley, Sunderland AFC's Player of the Century, recalls his first journey to the north-east from London on signing for the Black Cats from Millwall

TRAVELLING IN STYLE

During the 1920s Sunderland AFC used to own a railway carriage which was kept at Monkwearmouth station. It would be hitched up to the mainline trains when the team was travelling to away games.

Inside, the players enjoyed comparative luxury for the day and whiled away the hours playing cribbage on green baize tables. On the way back the players would take up the same position as the outward journey and if they won there was the added bonus of a packet of ten cigarettes waiting for each of them.

INTO THE LIGHT

On 1 December 1952 Sunderland travelled to The Dell to play Southampton in a friendly match. The game was significant because it was the first time that Sunderland had played under floodlights in England; 15,000 supporters witnessed an entertaining 3–2 victory.

Nine days later and it was Sunderland's turn to unveil the lights, with a visit from Dundee. The game was always entertaining and indeed a novelty for the 34,352 crowd. Surprisingly the Scots led at half time, despite Shackleton scoring the first goal of the game; however Sunderland eventually prevailed 5–3.

THEY SAID IT ...

'I don't scare easily and never did but I remember times when I was frightened of Alan Brown. A bollocking from him was like ten from anybody else.'
Brian Clough reveals then Sunderland manager Alan Brown's managerial style

'Johnny didn't say too much, but he was a gem and as hard as nails. In fact, he used to put Mickey Spillane detective novels down his socks as shin pads.'
Former Sunderland player George Mulhall reflects on his colleague Johnny Crossan's state of the art football equipment

'I can remember walking into the Sunderland dressing room for the first time and being introduced to people. Little Nicky Sharkey was there and when I was told he was the club's centre-forward, I burst out laughing!'
Scotland legend Jim Baxter's recipe for how to win friends and influence people on his first day at Sunderland AFC

'Jim could make his left foot talk. His right was just for standing on.'
Sunderland's George Kinnell gives his opinion on his cousin, Jim Baxter's, football ability

'I spoke to Stuart Pearson who had been a team mate of mine at Hull (City) and he told me not to worry about the game because the West Ham lads had been drinking all weekend after the Cup win.'
Ken Knighton, Sunderland's then manager, recalls the West Ham United players' pre-match training routine before the crucial promotion game at Roker Park in 1980 against the Hammers. They had won the FA Cup the previous Saturday, but unsurprisingly, Sunderland were the victors this time!

TRAGEDY

It is always tragic and sad when any person dies. They leave behind family and friends who mourn their passing. Sunderland AFC has had its share of footballers who have died young, who were at one time on, or while still on the Black Cats' books, some of course during the two world wars:

Name	Age at Death	Year of Death
James Logan	25	1896
Matthew Ferguson	29	1902
Jimmy Miller	36	1907
Arnie Davison	46	1910
William Gibson	43	1911
Ronald Brebner	33	1914
Leigh Richmond Roose	38	1916
Albert Milton	32	1917
Sandy McAllister	39	1918
Harry Low	38	1920
Jimmy Leslie	47	1920
English McConnell	43	1928
Jack Bartley	20	1929
George Payne	45	1932
Jimmy Thorpe	22	1936
Tom Wallace	32	1939
Billy Ellis	44	1939
Percy Saunders	25	1942
Reg Wilkinson	47	1953
David Wright	47	1946
Keith Hird	27	1967
Mel Holden	26	1981
Jim Holton	42	1993
Tim Gilbert	36	1995
Rob Hindmarch	41	2002
Tim Carter	40	2008

THE BOSS IS ALWAYS RIGHT!

Sunderland AFC have had 33 managers in its 130-year history (including Steve Bruce). Below is the league record of them all.

	Manager	Pld	W	D	L	F	A	Pts
1	Bob Kyle	746	342	139	265	1,355	1,138	823
2	Alan Brown	493	182	140	171	723	721	504
3	Bill Murray	469	166	132	171	753	807	464
4	Johnny Cochrane	449	187	107	155	849	762	481
5	Peter Reid	306	135	88	83	414	330	493
6	Alex Mackie	204	102	44	58	331	225	248
7	Denis Smith	201	79	56	66	293	269	293
8	Tom Watson	168	106	25	37	448	225	235
9	Bob Stokoe	166	77	41	48	241	159	197
10	Mick McCarthy	129	53	24	52	159	156	183
11	Alan Durban	112	31	34	47	114	158	127
12	Ian McColl	109	34	23	52	141	190	91
13	Bob Campbell	94	38	20	36	118	118	96
14	Roy Keane	94	41	16	37	119	121	139
15	Ken Knighton	80	33	19	28	115	91	83
16	Lawrie McMenemy	77	23	21	33	86	109	90
17	Jimmy Adamson	75	26	25	24	108	97	79
18	Mick Buxton	68	23	21	24	72	70	90
19	Len Ashurst	55	15	13	27	52	74	58
20	Malcolm Crosby	46	14	12	20	56	66	54
21	Terry Butcher	38	10	7	21	38	53	37
22	Directors	33	6	9	18	42	66	21
23	Billy Elliott	27	13	8	6	46	29	34
24	George Hardwick	27	13	3	11	44	38	29
25	Ricky Sbragia	23	5	6	12	21	30	21
26	Howard Wilkinson	20	2	5	13	15	33	11
27	Dave Merrington	12	6	3	3	22	14	15
28	Kevin Ball	10	1	2	7	7	18	5
29	Ian McFarlane	7	2	1	4	8	12	3
30	Niall Quinn	5	1	0	4	6	9	3
31	Mick Docherty	4	2	0	2	6	4	6
32	Bryan Robson	1	0	1	0	2	2	1

MANAGERS

The following is a précis of some of the managers who
Sunderland AFC have had at the helm.

Tom Watson
Watson was manager of Sunderland AFC when they entered
the Football League in 1890. He put together the Team Of
All The Talents and was widely regarded, at that time, as
being without peer. He eventually went to Liverpool where he
managed them to their very first Championship Trophy.

   Ironically, and rather touchingly, he is buried on Merseyside
next to another of our greats, John 'Teddy' Doig, the 'Prince
of Goalkeepers', who starred for SAFC and then Liverpool.
Watson is perhaps the best manager Sunderland AFC has ever
had.

Robert Campbell
Originally manager of our highly successful 'A' team, Robert
Campbell took over from Tom Watson in 1896, but fared
poorly to start with. In fact in his first season as boss, Sunderland
scored only 34 goals and played in end of season 'Test Matches'.
Bob's brother was the majestic Johnny Campbell who, to this
day, remains one of Sunderland AFC's greatest goalscorers,
with some 150 strikes. Curiously, Campbell had been offered
the manager's position at Newcastle United in 1895, but opted
to remain loyal to the red and whites.

Alex Mackie
From 1899 to 1905, the reign of Mackie was shrouded in
controversy. He was boss of Sunderland AFC during the
McCombie Affair when a £100 gift by SAFC was adjudged to
have infringed the FA's rule books. Alex was suspended from
football for three months, even though a court of law vindicated
the club in their assessment that a loan had been paid. He
remained undefeated in 171 of his 204 league games for the
club, a tremendous record. While suspended, it is unclear who
took charge of the team. Some say Fred Dale, but the best guess
would be that the directors stepped into the breach.

Bob Kyle

Sunderland's longest-serving manager, Kyle took over the reigns in 1905 and left in 1928 after 8,293 days and 746 league matches in charge. Originally from Belfast, he played for their Distillery Club as a goalkeeper from 1897 until his transfer to Sunderland. He applied for the job with over 70 other candidates. In time he would win one league championship for Sunderland and lead them to their first FA Cup Final. It is doubtful whether any manager has given so much to Sunderland AFC, and in his nineteen seasons, the football club would end in the top ten no fewer than thirteen times.

He was responsible for bringing such brilliant players as Holley, Thomson, Bridgett, Mordue, Ness and Cuggy to Wearside – immense talent. Perhaps the biggest bargain in the club's history was the deal that brought Bobby Gurney to Sunderland, for the paltry sum of £10. In 1912/13 he went very close to winning the double, a narrow FA Cup Final defeat by bogey team Aston Villa at Crystal Palace depriving him of that distinction. Kyle died in 1932, just four years after leaving SAFC, at the age of sixty-six. Some say that his departure from Sunderland AFC was all too much for him. The directors once more chose the team prior to the arrival of the next manager.

Johnny Cochrane

Apart from Bob Stokoe, it's hard to imagine any Sunderland AFC manager as popular as Johnny Cochrane. This could be explained by the fact that he presided over our very first FA Cup win in 1937. He was boss for eleven years (1928 to 1939), 449 league games and 3,949 days. When Bob Kyle left it was mooted that Major Frank Buckley would take his place and George Jobey (famously of Derby County) was first in line to replace him, but he turned the job down after he asked for conditions on training and control of staff and the directors refused to hand these powers to the secretary. So Johnny Cochrane arrived from St Mirren, with whom he had won the Scottish Cup. He brought with him trainer Andy Reid, and one of the best scouts in the business, Scotsman Sammy Blyth.

Cochrane had an immediate impact on the club and in the 1928/29 season he steered the club to fourth place. This was in part due to the arrival of two experienced Scots – Tommy

McInally arrived from Glasgow Celtic and Adam McLean from Aberdeen. This season also, of course, saw Dave Halliday set a new goalscoring record with 43 goals for the club, in the campaign. Johnny resigned on 3 March 1939, where once more the directors took control until the arrival of William Murray. While some historians credit George Crow with the intervening games its likely that his tenure was administrative rather than as manager.

Bill Murray

While history is vague, it appears that Bill's first game in charge of SAFC was on Good Friday 7 April 1939, against Everton. His SAFC record wasn't brilliant, but it was long, at 469 games. His tenure was of course punctuated by the Second World War and would last until 1957.

   He was boss in perhaps Sunderland AFC's last great period, a one that would be soured by the 'Mr Smith' financial irregularities scandal, from which the football club took some forty years to recover. Murray resigned along with trainer Bert Johnston in 1957, both of them having been with the club for thirty years. The £200 fine issued by the FA for Murray's part in the Mr Smith affair was adjudged draconian in the extreme. By the time Alan Brown arrived, Sunderland had employed just six managers in sixty-seven years.

Alan Brown

Alan Brown would enjoy two spells at Sunderland and it's fair to say that he had a rocky relationship with the crowd. While he will always be remembered as the man who presided over Sunderland's very first relegation, it should be pointed out that in truth he took over an ageing squad at a very traumatic time for the club. It is probably best to remember him as the man who provided the catalyst for one of the best youth set ups in the country, one that would pay handsome dividends come 1973. It is also largely forgotten that he had enjoyed a good playing career with Burnley, having featured for them in the 1947 FA Cup Final as captain against Charlton Athletic.

   He gained promotion for Sunderland in 1963/64 and then promptly left for Sheffield Wednesday. He returned in 1968 but presided over relegation in 1970. It is not a generally known fact, but when Brown took over in 1957 he was Sunderland's first English manager for over sixty years, since Tom Watson. He was only the seventh manager in our history. Brown died on 8 March 1996 at the age of eighty-one. A perfectly observed minute's silence prior to our game with Derby County in the final Roker Park season, the very next day, told its own story.

George Hardwick

Hardwick arrived on Wearside as a replacement for the departed manager, Alan Brown, well into the 1964/65 season. He didn't arrive until November, and with only one win under our belts, it proved to be a baptism of fire for the former Middlesbrough player. Indeed, Sunderland's first eleven away games of the campaign produced not one point. He guided the club to comparative safety, fifteenth, so avoiding the drop, but his departure really set the scene for a merry go round of managers. He lasted six months and was replaced by Ian McColl.

Ian McColl

McColl, the Scottish international boss, arrived at Sunderland for the start of the 1965/66 season. He immediately signed his fellow countryman and Rangers legend Slim Jim Baxter. However, the initial euphoria turned into a damp squib as his three seasons in charge produced some very mixed results and poor league placings.

Funnily enough he had more success on the youth front with the kids losing to Arsenal in the Youth Cup Final, although this might have had more to do with a certain Brian Clough who was in charge of the youngsters. Notable events included the introduction of Bobby Kerr to the senior side, a record Elland Road crowd turning up for the visit of SAFC in the FA Cup and the eventual demise of Charlie Hurley. An eventful tenure, but too often for the wrong reasons.

Bob Stokoe

Since his arrival in 1972, only two managers have served as Sunderland boss longer than Bob Stokoe – Denis Smith and Peter Reid. After the 1973 FA Cup semi-final victory at Hillsborough he famously quoted, 'I should pack it all in.

There'll never be another moment like it.' All of Wearside agreed with the above sentiments as after thirty-six long years the most prestigious domestic knockout club trophy in football travelled to Roker Park.

After managerial spells at Charlton Athletic, Rochdale, Bury, Carlisle United and Blackpool, whom incidentally he had led to victory in the Anglo-Italian tournament, the ex-Magpie succumbed to initial Sunderland defeat at the hands of Burnley. Sunderland then embarked on a run of thirty-two games, with only five defeats, culminating in a day that Wearside will never forget. Not bad for a side that started in the doldrums, defeated by Stoke at the first League Cup hurdle, and searching for only its fifth win in eighteen league attempts, on his arrival.

From fourth bottom they would end the season sixth, although at first an outbreak of flu threatened to scupper the season altogether. It is also pertinent to note that on Stokoe's arrival Sunderland hadn't bought a player for over two years. He promoted Sunderland in 1975/76 and then left the very next season, prematurely some say, as the club made a poor start to top-flight football. While he returned briefly to try and ultimately fail to sort out the mess left by McMenemy, technically presiding over our demise into the Third Division, the Sunderland fans can only remember this man with the greatest affection. Who can forget his famous trilby reappearing at Valley Parade for his first game back in charge. The greeting he received from the red and white faithful left you in no doubt what everyone thought.

However, to sum up Stokoe you always go back to the final whistle of the FA Cup semi-final against Arsenal at Hillsborough in 1973. The travelling Roker Roar refused to move until their 'Messiah' Bob Stokoe appeared. Taking the salute, he turned and went back to the dressing room; tears running down his cheeks.

Jimmy Adamson

He had played under former Sunderland manager Alan Brown during a spell at Burnley. To say that he took over the reigns at Roker Park with the team in a bit of a state was an understatement. They were struggling against relegation but Adamson came in and changed things around. A run of

nine consecutive defeats was halted on 22 January 1977 and
Sunderland went on to complete one of the most brilliant fight-
backs seen in modern-day football. In their last nineteen games,
Sunderland lost only three times. Adamson was replaced
as Sunderland manager by caretaker Dave Merrington on
26 October 1978, and would go on to take charge of Leeds
United.

Ken Knighton

Sunderland manager Ken Knighton played for six clubs during
his professional career – Wolverhampton Wanderers, Oldham
Athletic, Preston North End, Blackburn Rovers, Hull City and
Sheffield Wednesday. He also played under four managers at
Hillsborough – Stan Cullis, Andy Beattie, with whom he had
also had as his boss at Molineux, Terry Neill and Tommy
Docherty.

Knighton's playing career had ended in January 1976 and
Jimmy Adamson brought him to Wearside as coach in the
summer of 1978. When he took over the reins on 30 June
1979, he immediately recruited Frank Clark from Nottingham
Forest as his assistant and also brought Peter Eustace from
Hillsborough as coach. Knighton had a decent enough
managerial record at Sunderland, taking the Wearsiders up
to the First Division in the club's centenary season in 1979/80
after a famous win and never-to-be-forgotten night against FA
Cup winners West Ham United at Roker Park.

He was replaced by Mick Docherty on 12 April 1981, with
four games of the 1980/81 season left.

Alan Durban

Alan Durban arrived on Wearside in June 1981 and in time
became one of the most popular of the recent managers. His
first acquisition was a beauty, Ally McCoist, and it was such
a shame that an alleged falling out with the then Sunderland
chairman saw his demise in 1984. His 993-day reign saw us
gain our highest league placing since 1955/56 – thirteenth.
Statistically his record was little better than McMenemy's
but everyone could see what he was trying to achieve. There
appeared to be a purpose to his reign and he briefly returned to
assist Peter Reid in the backroom in the 1990s.

Len Ashurst

Taking over from caretaker Pop Robson, after the demise of Alan Durban for the last thirteen games of the 1983/84 campaign, Ashurst was no stranger to Wearside. With 401 league appearances in a red and white shirt, the fourth highest in Sunderland AFC's illustrious history, he had given stalwart service in a great defensive career. However, while he guided Sunderland to the 1985 Milk Cup Final and defeat by Norwich, relegation in the same season saw the writing on the wall for the former Newport County boss. His place was taken by Lawrie McMenemy.

Lawrie McMenemy

In July 1985 Lawrie McMenemy arrived on Wearside as a hero. Appointed by then chairman Tom Cowie after a fairly successful spell at Southampton in which he won the FA Cup in 1976, by the time he left Wearside in April 1987, it is fair to say that he was blamed for our relegation into the Third Division, even though Bob Stokoe took the reins for the last few games.

Reasons for any unpopularity though are probably not that simplistic. In 77 league games he won just 23. It's interesting to note that there were managers previous and since that had poorer records than 'Big Lawrie'.

It's fair to say that over twenty years since demotion to the third tier of English football, he remains extremely unpopular on Wearside.

Denis Smith

In placing Denis Smith's contribution to Sunderland AFC into perspective, one must realise that there are only six managers in the history of SAFC who have been in the hot seat for longer than the man recruited from York City in 1987. He promised us that he would get us out of the Third Division at the first attempt and did just that, along with his friend and club coach Viv Busby. Smith was an uncompromising but always honest footballer in his time with Stoke City, and his eventual demise on Wearside in December 1991 was inevitable but sad. He had a great empathy with the fans and is always well received on his return. His greatest find was Marco Gabbiadini, who between Rowell and Phillips was unquestionably the most exciting player to wear the red and white stripes.

Malcolm Crosby

South Shields-born Crosby was Sunderland to the core. He achieved a lifetime's ambition when he succeeded Denis Smith into the Roker Park hot seat in 1992. While he famously guided Sunderland AFC to that year's FA Cup Final against Liverpool, it has since become evident that his main strengths lie as a number two. He is widely regarded as an excellent coach. Perhaps more than anything his appointment as manager was due to media pressure; it wouldn't have looked good for a caretaker to lead the Black Cats out at Wembley way. His reign ended, typically for Sunderland, with an away Pools Panel defeat at Tranmere Rovers.

Terry Butcher

No player has given such stalwart service to the England national team than Terry Butcher. His famous exploits against Sweden, blood pouring from a head wound, typified his will to win and never-say-die attitude. Unfortunately for Sunderland, both his playing and managerial careers on Wearside never hit the heights.

Taking over from Malcolm Crosby at the beginning of 1993, Butcher, like his predecessor drifted into the managerial position. By May and a last-gasp defeat by Notts County at Meadow Lane, that nearly saw us back in the Third Division, something had to give. It did, Terry Butcher departed just a few months later to be replaced by Mick Buxton. He had achieved just 10 league victories in 38 attempts. The managerial merry-go-round on Wearside was reaching dizzying heights.

Mick Buxton

With Sunderland unable to attract a top name to the Wearside hot seat, Mick Buxton was given the job in what could be termed a panic measure. While he had enjoyed a respectable career in management it just didn't appear to be the one. In his first season in charge, 1993/94, he did, it has to be said, steady the rocky Roker ship, and the respectable twelfth place was far better than many dared hope for after the awful start.

However, the next campaign proved to be a bridge too far for Mick Buxton and with seven games left he departed to make way for Peter Reid.

Peter Reid

Peter Reid was born in Huyton, Liverpool on 20 June 1956. He would go on to enjoy a distinguished playing career with Bolton Wanderers, Everton, QPR and Manchester City before moving into management at Maine Road. During his spell with Bolton he played at Roker Park in a never-to-be-forgotten Easter Monday match in 1976, when Sunderland clinched promotion in front of a crowd of 51,983. He later said the atmosphere made 'a lasting impression' on him.

While Reid was a huge success at Bolton, it was as an Everton player that he is best remembered. The Toffees were arguably in their heyday in the 1980s when they collected two Championship titles and enjoyed success in Europe. He went on to be capped by England and was part of Bobby Robson's side in the 1986 World Cup finals in Mexico and played in the famous 'Hand of God' game against Argentina.

Reid played 535 League games, won the European Cup Winners' Cup, the FA Cup, appearing in three consecutive finals, and won the League Cup twice. He was also voted the Players' Player of the year in 1985. Reid's management record at Maine Road shows that he guided them to a top-six finish twice. He took charge at Roker Park on 29 March 1995 and guided Sunderland to safety in the remaining seven games of the season. He then went on to deliver the club's two best-placed top flight finished since the 1950s.

Howard Wilkinson

Regarded by the Sunderland support as an horrendous managerial appointment, the ex-England boss and FA technical supremo was an unpopular choice as Wearside boss, allegedly following a phone call from then chairman Bob Murray asking his opinion on who should be the new Sunderland boss (he nominated himself). He lasted a mere twenty league games in which he won two.

Mick McCarthy

Joined the club at a difficult time having endured the 19-point season in which Sunderland AFC were relegated and faced financial meltdown. He was given little in the way of transfer funds and did the best he could, however, it resulted in the 15-point season and broke a plethora of English football league records. He is still widely regarded as a decent manager by the Sunderland rank and file.

Kevin Ball

A Sunderland AFC legend having chalked up one of the highest appearance records for the club. A no-nonsense footballer, he was drafted in for the last few games of the 2005/06 season although it was the short straw with relegation staring the club in the face.

Niall Quinn

In the 130-year history of Sunderland AFC, Niall Quinn will be judged as one of the greatest characters ever. A player, manager and then chairman, his managerial reign lasted a mere five league games before he bowed to the inevitable and handed over to Roy Keane. You'll not find many saying anything but positive things about 'Quinny'. Quite simply, he's a legend.

Roy Keane

One of the greatest ever players that 'British' football has produced, Irishman Roy Keane arrived as a high-profile capture for the football club after an illustrious playing career, primarily with Manchester United. His appointment raised the profile of the club enormously as media interest grew to fever pitch.

Given seemingly unlimited funds by Sunderland AFC, he won promotion at the club's first attempt and then guided the club to safety in its first season back in the Premier League. However, trouble brewed and during the 2008/09 season he resigned following an alleged fall out with Sunderland's major shareholder, Texan Ellis Short.

After four months out of the game, he was appointed manager of Ipswich Town in April 2009.

Ricky Sbragia

Following the resignation of Roy Keane, Ricky Sbragia appeared an unwilling conscript into the bear pit that is the SAFC managerial position.

Initially he fared well, particularly with the drubbing of West Bromwich Albion at the Stadium of Light, but things gradually went downhill and he presided over just 5 wins in 23 Premier League games. However, his tenure had a successful ending as he kept Sunderland in the top flight, albeit by the failings of other teams, most notably arch-rivals Newcastle United who were relegated, as a prime reason.

He resigned immediately after Sunderland's last game of the 2008/09 Premier League season, a 3–2 defeat by third-placed Chelsea.

Steve Bruce

On 2 June 2009 Sunderland AFC officially announced that they had appointed Corbridge-born Steve Bruce to the manager's position at the Stadium of Light. It was immediately reported that the former Manchester United player would be given up to £40m to spend in the transfer market.

Although born in Northumberland, he grew up in Wallsend, home of the famous Boys' Club.

Sunderland AFC was Bruce's seventh managerial appointment having also been the boss at Sheffield United, Huddersfield Town, Wigan Athletic (twice), Crystal Palace and Birmingham City.

THEY SAID IT ...

'I'll wait all night to finish it.'

Referee George Courtney informs Sunderland goalkeeper Tony Norman that the Newcastle supporters' efforts to stop the 1990 play-off game (with their arch-rivals winning 2–0), by invading the pitch, would be in vain

HOW MUCH?

Although it is sometimes difficult to interpret the size of transfer fees due to some being undisclosed and the fact that some of the figures quoted are maximum amounts payable, under certain circumstances, it is fair to believe Sunderland AFC's record transfer dealings could be as follows:

Darren Bent	£16,500,000
Craig Gordon	£9,000,000
Anton Ferdinand	£8,000,000
Tore André Flo	£8,000,000
Lee Cattermole	£8,000,000
Kenwyne Jones	£6,000,000
Frazier Campbell	£6,000,000
Kieran Richardson	£5,500,000
Michael Chopra	£5,000,000
Lorik Cana	£5,000,000
George McCartney	£5,000,000
Claudio Reyna	£4,500,000
Emerson Thome	£4,500,000
Andy Reid	£4,000,000

The vast majority of the above have been signed since Niall Quinn became chairman of the club in 2006 with the backing of first the Drumaville Consortium and then the wealthy Texan-born Ellis Short, the current owner of Sunderland AFC. Ellis took control of the club in the summer of 2009.

THEY SAID IT

'He wanted to wear the red and white stripes so badly and that was the key for us on top of his natural ability, which goes without saying.'

Sunderland Chairman Niall Quinn on the signing of Darren Bent

'If a match were to played anywhere within 100 miles of the town the very spectators whom you are so anxious to get rid off would most certainly be present so we don't see that playing at a neutral venue would make any difference. In conclusion the conduct of your committee and players has rendered any further negotiations between us impossible and each club must stand or fall on its own merits.'

Sunderland AFC's curt reply to their arch rivals Sunderland Albion in 1889 as the war of words reached a crescendo, played out in the local newspapers

'The complaint preferred by Albion had reference to the alleged "brutal conduct" of the Sunderland spectators in the match Sunderland v Albion on January 12th last. The indictment set forth that the supporters of Albion and their umpire (Mr James Allan) were openly threatened on the field, that during the latter part of the game mud was thrown at the Albion players and their umpire, that the referee was hooted and howled at by the crowd whenever he gave a decision in favour of Albion, and that after the match the brake conveying the Albion players from the field was stoned, and several of the players, including their umpire were injured.'

An extract from the report into the going on during the local derby between Sunderland AFC and Sunderland Albion in 1889 indicating that the former had not, perhaps, been as hospitable as the visitors would have liked!

'The 1973 Cup win was a once-in-a century smile from the Gods. It remained inconceivable throughout. It was an entry into realms of unbelief.'

**Arthur Appleton, Sunderland AFC Historian,
The Story Of Sunderland, 1979**

'Mr Alan Brown's decision to part company from Sunderland Football Club will be welcomed by his critics, of whom he has more than his fair share. But those with the interests of the club at heart will be sorry to see him go.

Twice he has come to Sunderland's rescue to face the task of reviving the club's fortunes at a time when they were at a low ebb. If the team has failed to make much headway this season what must not be overlooked is that Mr Brown has had to rely upon the same talent which took Sunderland into 5th place last season. Nor can Mr Brown's contribution to the club finances – in two years £200,000 has been received in transfer fees – be ignored. In that same period no money has been available to buy players. Perhaps Sunderland has been guilty of undervaluing his services.'

The *Sunderland Echo* comment on the 1972 departure of Manager Alan Brown that brought about the appointment of Bob Stokoe

VANCOUVER ROYAL CANADIANS

When Sunderland appeared as the Vancouver Royal Canadians in the league sponsored by the United Soccer Association in 1967, the starting appearances, goalscorers, fixtures and results were as follows:

	Name	Appearances	Goals
1	Jim Montgomery	7	
2	Cecil Irwin	7	
3	John Parke	7	
4	Colin Todd	10	1
5	George Kinnell	11	2
6	Jim Baxter	11	2
7	Alan Gauden	6	2
8	John O'Hare	12	1
9	Neil Martin	12	2
10	George Herd	7	2
11	George Mulhall	9	3
12	Jimmy Shoulder	5	1
13	Derek Forster	5	
14	Colin Suggett	12	3
15	Brian Heslop	7	1
16	Billy Hughes	4	
	Total		20

Date	Fixture & Result			Crowd
28/5/1967	Golden Gate Gales	6–1	Vancouver RC	8,177
4/6/1967	Detroit Cougars	1–1	Vancouver RC	11,629
7/6/1967	Vancouver RC	4–1	Dallas Tornado	10,053
11/6/1967	Vancouver RC	1–0	Boston Rovers	7,616
14/6/1967	LA Wolves	5–1	Vancouver RC	5,251
18/6/1967	Vancouver RC	1–4	Houston Stars	6,785
21/6/1967	Vancouver RC	2–4	Toronto City	5,114
25/6/1967	Toronto City	2–2	Vancouver RC	4,385
28/6/1967	Washington Whips	1–1	Vancouver RC	8,709
1/7/1967	Chicago Mustangs	2–2	Vancouver RC	3,602
5/7/1967	Vancouver RC	1–1	New York Skyliners	6,533
8/7/1967	Vancouver RC	3–1	Cleveland Stokers	6,012

At the end of the tournament and in true American style an All Star Team was chosen from the 12 that took part. Sunderland had one representative in the following line-up:

USA All-Star Team

Position	Name	Team
Goalkeeper	Bobby Clark	Washington Whips
Defence	Mario Tito	Houston Stars
Defence	Jose Fidelis	Houston Stars
Defence	Pat Stanton	Toronto City
Midfield	Jim Baxter	Vancouver Royal Canadians
Midfield	Tommy McMillan	Washington Whips
Midfield	Ary Clemente	Houston Stars
Forward	Paulo Borges	Houston Stars
Forward	Peter Dobing	Cleveland Stokers
Forward	George Eastham	Cleveland Stokers
Forward	Roy Vernon	Cleveland Stokers

THE CASE AGAINST BILBAO?

Watch a live Athletic Club Bilbao La Liga game on, say, Sky Television and the chances are that at some point the commentator will tell you that the Basque team wear their red and white stripes (*rojiblancos*), black shorts and black socks in homage to Sunderland AFC, or most definitively Arthur Pentland, a British migrant worker from the north-east of England who was a founding member of the club. The questions posed over the years are 'who was Arthur Pentland?' and 'how come Athletic wear red and white stripes?'

To assist with answering the above questions we must first look at the origins of Athletic Bilbao. Football was introduced to Bilbao by two distinct groups of players, both with British connections. In the late nineteenth century Bilbao was a leading port at the heart of an important industrial area with iron mines and shipyards nearby. It was the driving force of the Spanish economy and as a result attracted many migrant workers. Among them were miners from the north-east of England, including Sunderland, and shipyard workers from Southampton and Portsmouth. In the early 1890s these workers came together and formed Bilbao Football Club.

Meanwhile, sons of the Basque educated classes had made the opposite journey and went to Britain to complete their studies in civil engineering and commerce. While in Britain these students developed an interest in football and on their return to Bilbao they began to arrange games with British workers.

In 1898 students belonging to the Gymnasium Zamacois founded the Athletic Club, deliberately using the English spelling. In 1901 a meeting was held in the Café Garcia which established more formal rules and regulations.

In 1902 the two Bilbao clubs entered a combined team, known as Club Vizcaya, in the first Copa Del Rey. They returned with the trophy after defeating FC Barcelona in the final. This would lead to the eventual merger of the two clubs as Athletic Club de Bilbao in 1903. In the same year Basque students also formed Athletic Club de Madrid, this club later evolving into Atlético Madrid.

Athletic Club Bilbao's actual foundation date is a subject of debate among football historians. The club itself declares 1898, but others claim 1901 is the true founding year.

Equally debated is the origin of the club colours. Although their first colours were blue and white stripes, in 1910 they switched to red and white stripes for the Vizcaya cup match against Sporting Irún on 9 January. There are three schools of thought about why this occurred. The most common theory is that they were changed out of deference to Sunderland and Southampton. Another is that an Athletic member was sent to Britain to buy a batch of blue and white tops but could not find any and returned with red and white ones instead.

Perhaps the most credible theory, however, is that red and white striped tops were the cheapest stripes to make because the same combination was used to make bed mattresses. The leftover cloth was easily converted into football shirts. Although both Athletic Bilbao and Atlético Madrid started out with blue and white stripes, the discovery of a cheaper option probably persuaded them to change. The Madrid club did it first and they became known as Los Colchoneros – The Mattress Makers.

There is a final version but not commonly referred to. The Basque flag is known as the Irukkina and was created in 1894 by Sabino Arana (the founder of Basque Nationalism). The red in the flag represented the blood shed by the Basques in defence of their land and the white represented God/the Catholic Church.

But what of Arthur Pentland? There is no known record of this man and, indeed, even if he was a founder of the Bilbao club the fact that they changed to red and white stripes in 1910 lends to a theory that he had nothing to do with the switch, as the foundation and the strip change came years after each other. Far more plausible is that there is a mix-up here with Fred Pentland who was the revered English manager of Athletic Bilbao from 1922 to 1933.

On 1 February 1941 General Franco, the Spanish dictator, forced the Basques to change the football club's name to Athletico Bilbao. However, by 1942/43 the club had effectively ignored this dictat and were back to calling themselves by the Anglicised Athletic. As if to emphasise the connection between the Basques and England, many volunteers from America, Ireland and Britain fought alongside the Basques in defence of the Spanish Republic against Franco's Nationalists. Indeed they formed what was known as the XV International Brigade.

The animosity between the peoples of the Republic and the Nationalists from Madrid remains to this day. Also remaining is the Basques' love of the English, as borne out by England being based in Bilbao for the 1982 World Cup. Although fiercely partisan, the Basque region, and Bilbao in particular, is known as a very friendly welcoming place and has taken on a sophisticated mode with culture being personified in the Guggenheim Museum that dominates part of the Bilbao skyline.

In about 1999 Sunderland AFC officially approached the Bilbao club's directors about various issues, including the above but they were non-plussed as to their links with our famous red and white stripes. In short, they'd never heard of us!

As it stands there is no connection between Sunderland AFC's red and white stripes and those of Bilbao and no historical evidence to support an Arthur Pentland influencing the famous strip of both teams. The most plausible explanation for the strips of both Bilbao and Atletico Madrid is due to the mattress makers. Nice story though. . . .

THE BLACK CATS

A perennial question for Sunderland fans has been the origin of the club's nickname, the Black Cats. In 2000 the club conducted a poll on what should be the club's official nickname.

It was a vote that came as something of a surprise to seasoned observers and historians of the club as the original nickname was considered to be the Black Cats for as long as anyone could remember. However, the vote was necessary as unofficial nicknames such as the Rokerites had emerged during the 1980s and 1990s.

The Black Cats nickname won in the vote – predictably and historically fittingly – by a landslide. The club then proceeded to define why they had become known as the Black Cats, and their version of there having been a gun battery at the mouth of the River Wear named 'The Black Cat' in the eighteenth century, provided an illuminating and hitherto unknown connection.

There is an alternative version that answers two basic questions:

1. Why did we adopt the name of the Black Cats?
2. When did we adopt the name of the Black Cats?

The picture of the original black cat was taken by Culshaw of Sunderland. Culshaw was responsible for taking other photographs of Sunderland AFC-related topics, such as team and player shots from around the turn of the twentieth century to about 1913.

A famous picture of the day shows Sunderland player Billy Hogg and two unnamed team-mates sitting at a table with a black cat being lovingly handled by them. It is the first known picture of a black cat being associated with Sunderland AFC. Hogg signed for Sunderland in 1899 making his debut against Notts County in December of that year. His last game for Sunderland AFC was on 17 April 1909, a 4–2 away win at Bristol City. We can therefore logically conclude that the black cat was officially adopted by Sunderland AFC's players in between that period, although Hogg did go onto be associated with Sunderland in a coaching capacity well into the 1920s and beyond.

A second and much rarer surviving image was believed to have been drawn by a young Sunderland fan in 1909. We can date it to 1909 because there is reference to the clubs that Sunderland AFC defeated in their 1908/09 FA Cup run. Therefore we can definitely prove that by the end of the 1908/09 campaign the nickname 'The Black Cats' had been formally adopted by the football club.

The alternative version of why Sunderland AFC adopted the nickname of the Black Cats is as follows. In January 1909, Sunderland were going through what was for them a relatively lean spell. It had been seven years since they had won the League, and the team which was to win the Championship with a record number of points and get to the Cup Final in 1913 was only just starting to come together.

A 4–1 home defeat to Liverpool on New Year's Day 1909 left the club in the bottom half of the First Division. When the players came into the dressing room the following day, before the game against Bury, they found a stray black cat in residence.

Sunderland defeated Bury 3–1, despite Harry Low missing a penalty, and this coincidence started the 'lucky black cat' story. A fortnight later when Sunderland went to Bramall Lane and won 3–2 in the FA Cup after being 0–2 down in the second half, the feline mascot was officially adopted by the players.

By the end of January 1909, the *Sunderland Echo* reported of the cat: 'there has been a big demand for its portrait, more having been disposed of than of all the players put together.' The thousands who went to Newcastle for the FA Cup quarter-final that season had black cat mascots adorned with red and white ribbons.

While the Black Cat Gun Battery story is a lovely historic backdrop, it would appear as though there is a rival to that account.

SUNDERLAND'S COMPLETE LEAGUE RECORD 1890 TO 2009

C = CHAMPIONS   P = PROMOTED   R = RELEGATED

Season	Div	P	W	D	L	F	A	Pts	Pos	
1890/91	D1	22	10	5	7	51	31	23	7	
1891/92	D1	26	21	0	5	93	36	42	1	C
1892/93	D1	30	22	4	4	100	36	48	1	C
1893/94	D1	30	17	4	9	72	44	38	2	
1894/95	D1	30	21	5	4	80	37	47	1	C
1895/96	D1	30	15	7	8	52	41	37	5	
1896/97	D1	30	7	9	14	34	47	23	15	
1897/98	D1	30	16	5	9	43	30	37	2	
1898/99	D1	34	15	6	13	41	41	36	7	
1899/1900	D1	34	19	3	12	50	35	41	3	
1900/01	D1	34	15	13	6	57	26	43	2	
1901/02	D1	34	19	6	9	50	35	44	1	C
1902/03	D1	34	16	9	9	51	36	41	3	
1903/04	D1	34	17	5	12	63	49	39	6	
1904/05	D1	34	16	8	10	60	44	40	5	
1905/06	D1	38	15	5	18	61	70	35	14	
1906/07	D1	38	14	9	15	65	66	37	10	
1907/08	D1	38	16	3	19	78	75	35	16	
1908/09	D1	38	21	2	15	78	63	44	3	
1909/10	D1	38	18	5	15	66	51	41	8	
1910/11	D1	38	15	15	8	67	48	45	3	
1911/12	D1	38	14	11	13	58	51	39	8	
1912/13	D1	38	25	4	9	86	43	54	1	C
1913/14	D1	38	17	6	15	63	52	40	7	
1914/15	D1	38	18	5	15	81	72	41	8	
1919/20	D1	42	22	4	16	72	59	48	5	
1920/21	D1	42	14	13	15	57	60	41	12	
1921/22	D1	42	16	8	18	60	62	40	12	

Season	Div	P	W	D	L	F	A	Pts	Pos	
1922/23	D1	42	22	10	10	72	54	54	2	
1923/24	D1	42	22	9	11	71	54	53	3	
1924/25	D1	42	19	10	13	64	51	48	7	
1925/26	D1	42	21	6	15	96	80	48	3	
1926/27	D1	42	21	7	14	98	70	49	3	
1927/28	D1	42	15	9	18	74	76	39	15	
1928/29	D1	42	20	7	15	93	75	47	4	
1929/30	D1	42	18	7	17	76	80	43	9	
1930/31	D1	42	16	9	17	89	85	41	11	
1931/32	D1	42	15	10	17	67	73	40	13	
1932/33	D1	42	15	10	17	63	80	40	12	
1933/34	D1	42	16	12	14	81	56	44	6	
1934/35	D1	42	19	16	7	90	51	54	2	
1935/36	D1	42	25	6	11	109	74	56	1	C
1936/37	D1	42	19	6	17	89	87	44	8	
1937/38	D1	42	14	16	12	55	57	44	8	
1938/39	D1	42	13	12	17	54	67	38	16	
1946/47	D1	42	18	8	16	65	66	44	9	
1947/48	D1	42	13	10	19	56	67	36	20	
1948/49	D1	42	13	17	12	49	58	43	8	
1949/50	D1	42	21	10	11	83	62	52	3	
1950/51	D1	42	12	16	14	63	73	40	12	
1951/52	D1	42	15	12	15	70	61	42	12	
1952/53	D1	42	15	13	14	68	82	43	9	
1953/54	D1	42	14	8	20	81	89	36	18	
1954/55	D1	42	15	18	9	64	54	48	4	
1955/56	D1	42	17	9	16	80	95	43	9	
1956/57	D1	42	12	8	22	67	88	32	20	
1957/58	D1	42	10	12	20	54	97	32	21	R
1958/59	D2	42	16	8	18	64	75	40	15	
1959/60	D2	42	12	12	18	52	65	36	16	
1960/61	D2	42	17	13	12	75	60	47	6	
1961/62	D2	42	22	9	11	85	50	53	3	
1962/63	D2	42	20	12	10	84	55	52	3	
1963/64	D2	42	25	11	6	81	37	61	2	P

Season	Div	P	W	D	L	F	A	Pts	Pos	
1964/65	D1	42	14	9	19	64	74	37	15	
1965/66	D1	42	14	8	20	51	72	36	19	
1966/67	D1	42	14	8	20	58	72	36	17	
1967/68	D1	42	13	11	18	51	61	37	15	
1968/69	D1	42	11	12	19	43	67	34	17	
1969/70	D1	42	6	14	22	30	68	26	21	R
1970/71	D2	42	15	12	15	52	54	42	13	
1971/72	D2	42	17	16	9	67	57	50	5	
1972/73	D2	42	17	12	13	59	49	46	6	
1973/74	D2	42	19	9	14	58	44	47	6	
1974/75	D2	42	19	13	10	65	35	51	4	
1975/76	D2	42	24	8	10	67	36	56	1	C
1976/77	D1	42	11	12	19	46	54	34	20	R
1977/78	D2	42	14	16	12	67	59	44	6	
1978/79	D2	42	22	11	9	70	44	55	4	
1979/80	D2	42	21	12	9	69	42	54	2	P
1980/81	D1	42	14	7	21	52	53	35	17	
1981/82	D1	42	11	11	20	38	58	44	19	
1982/83	D1	42	12	14	16	48	61	50	16	
1983/84	D1	42	13	13	16	42	53	52	13	
1984/85	D1	42	10	10	22	40	62	40	21	R
1985/86	D2	42	13	11	18	47	61	50	18	
1986/87	D2	42	12	12	18	49	59	48	20	R
1987/88	D3	46	27	12	7	92	48	93	1	C
1988/89	D2	46	16	15	15	60	60	63	11	
1989/90	D2	46	20	14	12	70	64	74	6	P
1990/91	D1	38	8	10	20	38	60	34	19	R
1991/92	D2	46	14	11	21	61	65	53	18	
1992/93	D1	46	13	11	22	50	64	50	21	
1993/94	D1	46	19	8	19	54	57	65	12	
1994/95	D1	46	12	18	16	41	45	54	20	
1995/96	D1	46	22	17	7	59	33	83	1	C
1996/97	PR	38	10	10	18	35	53	40	18	R
1997/98	D1	46	26	12	8	86	50	90	3	
1998/99	D1	46	31	12	3	91	28	105	1	C

Season	Div	P	W	D	L	F	A	Pts	Pos	
1999/2000	PR	38	16	10	12	57	56	58	7	
2000/01	PR	38	15	12	11	46	41	57	7	
2001/02	PR	38	10	10	18	29	51	40	17	
2002/03	PR	38	4	7	27	21	65	19	20	R
2003/04	D1	46	22	13	11	62	45	79	3	
2004/05	C	46	29	7	10	76	41	94	1	C
2005/06	PR	38	3	6	29	26	69	15	20	R
2006/07	C	46	27	7	12	76	47	88	1	C
2007/08	PR	38	11	6	21	36	59	39	15	
2008/09	PR	38	9	9	20	34	54	36	16	